THE
BORN-AGAIN JESUS

OF THE
WORD-FAITH TEACHINGS

By Judith A. Matta

Spirit of Truth Ministries
223 S. Magnolia, Fullerton, CA 92633

Dedication

To Irenaeus, who went before us with the
Spirit of Truth,
with thanksgiving to God for his life and
writings.

Contents

Preface

It is with a profound sense of gratitude and thanksgiving to God that I am able to present this study after three years of intensive research of the Word-Faith teachings. For ten years, my husband and I have pondered the problem posed by these teachings. Only during the last three years, after directing a specific prayer to the Lord, did we have answers to the dilemma in two words: Gnosticism and Irenaeus. The first was a heresy, and the second was a bishop who exposed that heresy during the First Century. From there, a simple prayer, this work has evolved.

In our years of walking with the Lord as Christians, we have noted several characteristics unique to the Word-Faith teaching and its adherents. It is these characteristics that initially warned us of its departure from true Christianity. Word-Faith teachers are dynamic and charismatic in presenting this system of success. Word-Faith rallies at large churches and convention centers serve to exercise their false sense of spiritual power with confession of desired results, whether financial or physical. Personally, they seem to have a confidence in themselves and in their accepting audience. This teaching breeds an intolerance for human weakness, and a lack of compassion. There appears to be no repentant heart or humble spirit before the Lord. Instead of worship-services, they hold rallies of self-motivation. There is no reverance before God, but there is a brash confrontation with a god whom they consider to be their equal. In recognizing these qualities, we had to ascertain that there were non-Christian elements to the Word-Faith teaching. At this point in time, I became aware of the books of E. W. Kenyon, and discovered in these writings the key to the foundational concepts behind Word-Faith teachings. It is then that the Holy Spirit gave me the answers of Gnosticism and Irenaeus. What had been previously discerned spiritually became visible heresy, and from there, could be analyzed and compared to Christian Scripture and doctrine.

The Word-Faith teaching is perhaps the most subtle heretical system to emerge in our own times. Many thousands in Christian churches have been subject to, or enticed by its call to wealth and prosperity. The spiritual blessings of Abraham's Covenant have been translated into physical abundance, as these teachings push believers into asking - no, demanding - what they want from God. However, Christians have been called to so much more, for our blessings through Jesus Christ and His salvation are what the prophets and Israel longed to see in their times. But the preoccupation of Word-Faith teachings is not with the spiritual blessings from God, but with wresting the physical goods of this world from Satan. This teaching justifies the fleshly desires of Mankind; those who have desires for things of this world can justify their worldly desires with allegedly "christian" doctrines. The Word-Faith teaching is a NEW, SECULAR MOVEMENT that has been presented to Christians from pulpits and the media.

There is a new term on the psychological scene; it is the term, "Tough Love." This kind of love is the love of a parent which does what is best for the child, no matter the cost emotionally to the parent, and sometimes at the expense of temporarily losing the affections of that child. This is a love that lasts - that is unconditional and based on Truth. Its opposite is a care-less love; a love that is concerned with peace at all costs, never mind the consequences. With this misunderstanding of love, Christians have been reluctant to speak out against any teaching for fear of being called "unloving," or "judgmental." It is a love that the Apostle Paul would know nothing about. At the risk of being called divisive, those that care about the Church have a duty to speak out when there is a false presentation of Jesus Christ and His Atonement. Christ is the **very foundation** - the Cornerstone upon which Christianity rests. A false understanding of the Person of Christ causes the whole church to collapse into rival factions, competing for power. This is the case regarding Word-Faith teachings that are being taught within the context of Christianity. Real love will speak to the teaching, while praying that the proponents of this teaching will be turned from it unto life everlasting.

Mrs. Judith Anne Matta
Fullerton, California
February 20, 1984

Introduction

The following study is concerned with the Word-Faith teaching made popular by many evangelists and teachers in the Christian churches today. These doctrines have found their way into pulpits and television by using many common, scriptural terms and ideas which sound "christian," but put a sword to the heart of biblical basics. By introducing laws which replace God's Grace, by presenting another "Jesus," not found in scripture, and by insisting that only those who follow them can "know" true faith, they have created dissension and friction among believers and disintegrated Christian worship communities.

Many have attempted to explain the problems presented by the Word-Faith movement, but the foundational doctrines have not been examined by any of these studies. This book is designed to introduce the reader to a thorough examination of the Word-Faith teaching as originated by E. W. Kenyon. Kenyon died in 1948, but his writings are still used by those who present his doctrines. Kenyon provides clear definitions of his systems used so often by the Word-Faith proponents. For this reason, the following study will use Kenyon more than any other source to explain the underlying assumptions of this teaching.

The foundations of the Word-Faith teaching are found in the ancient heresy of Gnosticism which appeared along with Christianity in the First Century. Gnosticism means "knowledge," in the Greek language. Knowledge was the primary tool that this heresy used, as it asserted that Man could become divine through the special knowledge of myths, incantations and rituals, some of which closely resembled Christian scripture and rituals.

Irenaeus, A bishop familiar with Gnostic teachings in Rome, gave to the Christians there a clear exposition of Gnostic teachings in a series of letters. Bishop Irenaeus exposed the mythology of Gnosticism disguised as it was, in Christian terms. He used the Word of God to argue orthodox, Christian doctrine. His letters appear together in volumes entitled "Against Heresy."

According to Irenaeus, and others writing against Gnosticism, Simon the Magician began this strange philosophy. He was the Simon presented in the Acts of the Apostles - one who desired the power of the Holy Spirit by offering money for it. Simon's mixture of Greek myths and Christian custom spread from Samaria into the cities surrounding the Mediterranean Sea. While in Rome, Irenaeus became familiar with various schools of Gnosticism; each had their own "master teacher" and mythological system. When Gnostics mingled with Christians in their assemblies, they adopted Christian terms and parodied orthodox doctrines. However, privately they taught their incantations and rituals to those who weren't satisfied with the Gospel of Jesus Christ. Many were not willing to face martyrdom in the Roman arenas, or the hardships associated with being Christian. For these, the Gnostic rejection of the Cross and suffering Savior provided a theological "escape." There is no reason to suffer for and because of a savior who had avoided suffering, Himself. Some Gnostic "gospels" describe a "laughing savior" who floated above his physical body that was on the Cross. Others taught that Jesus had no real, physical body.

Irenaeus knew the seductiveness of their "secret" sayings and self-assured arrogance. His writings contain interesting accounts of meetings between Christian leaders and Gnostic teachers. These meetings reflect the disgust that this heresy stirred in the hearts of those who guided the First-Century Christians. One such occurrance was between the Apostle John and a Gnostic teacher entering a public bath. John was clearly offended by his presence and exclaimed, "Let us flee this place lest any water that washes off of him fall upon us!"

Polycarp, who led Irenaeus to faith in Jesus Christ, met Valentinus, the head of the major Gnostic school in Rome.Full of self-importance, Valentinus said to Polycarp, "Do you know who I am?" Polycarp replied," Yes, I know that you are a son of Satan." There is little doubt that these Gnostics were not accepted by the elders or apostles as "christian" in any way. They made no compromises with either Gnostic doctrine or its advocates.

What distressed Irenaeus most was the fact that many Christians did not recognize Gnostics as heretical in their teaching. He compared it to the difference between cut glass and real emeralds. Their views

are full of blasphemies, he told the early
Christians, "Like poison disguised as
milk." With only one or two central issues
perverted - the identity of Jesus Christ or
the definition of "God" - the pure "milk of
the Word" is poisoned, and the whole
becomes intolerable to Christian belief.

In these last days, cults proliferate in
every society. Even Christians are being
drawn away, especially those who have not
taken time to read the scriptures and
follow the Holy Spirit in daily living,
enticed back into legalism in one form or
another. Most Christians do not realize
that cult members almost always have better
knowledge of certain scriptures which
appear to back their own assertions than
they do. They have, however, redefined
Christian terms. "Apples" may be the word
used by cult members, but oranges are being
presented, to put it simply. Other signs
of a cultish teaching are that it
downplays the role of Jesus Christ. He is
never the central figure, and is almost
always misrepresented as a mere Man. Cults
claim a possession of "real truth" which no
one else is teaching. Groups within
Christian churches which claim to have
deeper knowledge about spiritual truths
than other Christians or the pastor, are
sure participants in some form of cultish
teaching. However, even with these
familiar points in mind, scripture presents
another important point to remember.

In First John (4:1-6), the Holy Spirit
gives us guidelines by which to judge
whether a teaching is from Him or not. Any
teaching which is not of God is certainly

of the spirit of anti-Christ which is preparing the world to worship Satan. John writes, "Beloved, do not believe every spirit, but test the spirits to see whether they are from God; because many false prophets have gone out into the world. By this you know the Spirit of God: every spirit that confesses that Jesus Christ has come in the flesh is from God; and every spirit that does not confess Jesus is not from God; and this is the spirit of the antichrist, of which you have heard that it is coming, and now it is already in the world. You are from God, little children, and have overcome them; because greater is He who is in you than he who is in the world. They are from the world; THEREFORE THEY SPEAK AS FROM THE WORLD, AND THE WORLD LISTENS TO THEM. WE ARE FROM GOD; HE WHO KNOWS GOD LISTENS TO US; HE WHO IS NOT FROM GOD DOES NOT LISTEN TO US. BY THIS WE KNOW THE SPIRIT OF TRUTH AND THE SPIRIT OF ERROR." (NASB) Most Christians are aware that teachers must present Jesus Christ incarnate "in the flesh," but some have neglected to notice that tremendous popularity will follow those who are preaching another, worldly gospel. The world hates the true Gospel of a Crucified Savior and Risen Lord. They do not hunger for the things of God, but for what the world has to offer. Glamourous ministries are uncomfortable with heavenly rewards for earthly faith. Kenyon's gospel redefines "faith" to mean believing that what is spoken will be brought about in this life. His carbon-copy followers instruct Christians from television and radio programs in their "legal rights," without mention of Grace or dependance on Jesus

Christ. The reasons for their assertions will become clear as the Holy Spirit enlightens His Word to His own.

Chapter 1

Gnosticism: Ancient and New

Ancient Gnosticism

The ancient Gnostics taught a complete world-view differing entirely from that of the scriptures. In scripture, both Old and New Testaments, God is clearly in control of the physical world and the history of Mankind. He continually injects His Word through the Prophets and leaders of Israel in order to form them as a people obedient to Him.

Dualism, a black-and-white view of spiritual reality is foundational to all Gnosticism. The Gnostics saw the physical world as Evil. Only Spirit was good, untouched by material elements. Because of this, they either made themselves strangers to the world altogether, or used physical things with complete abandon. The monastic movement typified the former reaction to Evil in the world. Gnostics who participated in the sensuality of the world with abandon, sanctified themselves with ceremonies, preventing any touch of Evil upon them during their escapades. In either interpretation, the world continued to be intrinsically Evil, including all flesh. By separating a "Good" God from the Evil World, they could explain the Age-Old dilemma of the presence of Evil in a world created by a God Who is Good. All of these concepts are vitally important in understanding the Gnostic teachings being presented today - in the Word-Faith teaching especially.

The goal of the Gnostic was to release the "inner," spiritual man from his material world and self so that he would attain to his original, divinity. The necessary step in this attainment was Knowledge, both about the transcendent God and about himself. There were sacramental and mythological teachings which gave the Gnostic the abilities to render himself equal with the highest God in all aspects. Through rituals which imitated Baptism and Marriage, he could escape the evil forces that govern the World and rise above material things to the things of Pure Spirit and total power. In their system, Jesus was a "revealer" of the Way in attaining to this Purity; He revealed both the existence of the rift between the Highest God and the Evil world and the opposition of the Spirit and the Flesh. Through knowledge of the "secret sayings" of Jesus and others, the Gnostic traveled through a gauntlet of gods and forces into the realm of Goodness and Light.

The basic assertions above are common to most of the schools of Gnosticism which appeared soon after the establishment of the Christian churches in the Mediterranean area. Its origins, at least those given to us by Irenaeus and writers of his time, are found in the teachings of Simon the Magician. He claimed to have been the incarnation of the highest God. His mistress, Helen, was a reincarnation of the mystical Mother-goddess found in most Gnostic mythologies. The Male-Female dualism in the gods are necessary to

Gnosticism: Ancient and New

generate the other gods and forces, including Man.

There are two gods which have involved themselves with Mankind in Gnostic thought. The first is the god of Creation - sometimes called "Jehovah"- and the second is the Father of Jesus Christ. To the Gnostic, the death of Jesus was his escape from the god of this Creation, Evil or lesser in deity, into the Light of the Good God, Who became His Father. He would show the Way to oneness with this God. In order to reconcile their dualistic idea of God with scripture and orthodox interpretations, the Gnostics separated almost every attribute of the Godhead, creating countless forces and "gods." They tore God into little parts and pieces - Wisdom, and Purity, for example - and each part became a personality, force, or god to be used in controlling the Gnostic's rise to divinity.

Their mythologies wove scriptural themes with Greek concepts, but the end of the philosophy was oriental in substance. The battles of light and darkness, opposing forces of Good and Evil are all products of an Oriental mentality.

Because the god of Creation is the god of Israel presented in the Old Testament, the evil character of this god contaminates the Old Testament revelation making it lesser, and in some cases, totally without value to the Gnostic believer. The virtue of Wisdom in the book of Proverbs is a god unto itself; in some teachings, it is associated with the Serpent in the Garden of Eden. He guided Adam and Eve into Knowledge of Good and Evil, which was necessary for their escape the jealous god of Creation.

Irenaeus speaks of these separations in his letters. They are divisions between the Word and God, Christ and the Word, and Jesus from the Christ. By creating these divisions, Gnostics were able to insert their own definitions of each entity. The divided sections became heirarchies of forces in operation, evil if they are connected with this world and good if they belong to the highest God. However, the fascination of Gnosticism is not with God or gods, but with Man, and the individual, in particular. It is Man-centered and self-centered. The Gnostic molds his idea of god around a projection of his idea of Self and Good. God is an ideal who can be known and controlled by Man through Knowledge.

Another aspect that flows from their concept of god, especially the god of Creation, leads many to conclude that Oriental thought conceived Gnosticism. There is a definite anti-Jewish cast to the teachings. This "Jehovah" actually "learned" from Jesus about the highest God. Jehovah was the Judge, a role which denied his mercy.

The Spiritual Elite

One recently discovered text of Gnostic origins is called "Allogenes;" Allogenes means "Stranger" in English, describing one who is spiritually above and beyond this world of Evil. The writer saw himself as "one out of a thousand, two out of ten thousand." Humility was not part of their spirituality! Not only were they strangers from the world, but they remained strangers among themselves. Each teacher would personally instruct his students in his revelation from above. Irenaeus writes:"They consider themselves 'mature,' so that no one can be compared with them in the greatness of their Knowledge, not even if you mention Peter or Paul or any of the other apostles,...They...imagine that they...have discovered more than the apostles, and that the apostles preached the Gospel under the influence of Jewish opinions, but that they themselves are wiser and more intelligent than the apostles. (I,xiii,6)

In the hands of Gnostic teachers, apprentices were captive to arrogance:"If anyone yields himself to them like a little sheep, and follows out their practice and their redemption, such a person becomes so puffed up that he...walks with a strutting gait and a supercilious countenance, possessing all the pompous air of a cock!" (III,xv,2)

But Irenaeus detested most of all, their theft of God's Grace:"They desire to have in their possession, as their own property, the Grace that is from God above. (I,iv).

New Gnosticism

At the turn of the century, Gnostic sects had become a part of religious history in our own country. Mormonism, making gods of Man, and Christian Science, with its method of oneness with the Divine Mind, were both established the previous century. Mythology in Mormonism and "laws" in Christian Science were direct reflections of Gnostic thought. Jehovah's Witnesses have many Gnostic concepts, also.

Gnosticism has appealed to scholars in our own century who felt that history could give further answers to the mystery of Faith in Jesus Christ as presented in the Bible. They looked to ancient, Gnostic sects to provide insight and explanation for some of the difficulties found in the Epistles and the Gospel of John. Difficulties, for the scholars, were many. The natural mind cannot grasp the meaning of the scriptures without the Holy Spirit's enlightenment. The "war" between Flesh and Spirit could not be reconciled in the minds of philosophers like Rudolf Bultmann, who used Gnostic explanations of Pauline Epistles. He wrote that,"We cannot help but see...the relationships between Paul's thought and Greek mysticism (Gnosticism). Paul's views of Flesh and Spirit possess the dualism of (Gnosticism)."

He asserted that myths prevailed among early Christians and that scriptures must be "de-mythologized." The Resurrection and Virgin Birth were two of these so-called "myths," and his efforts left the scriptures in ruins. Still, the question persists today (which he introduced along with others): Is Gnosticism merely a sect of Christianity or is it heresy that departs from Christian doctrine altogether? As we have seen, the apostles and early leaders of the church had no problem responding negatively with fervor!

The later movement of existentialists, whose philosophy examined the "self" within, also provided a climate for the rise of Gnosticism in this century. But the German philosophers' "super-race" of elite Knowers was the philosophical idea that moved Hitler into a climate of power. The ancient Gnostics and their counterparts in this century have translated the desire to control Self and Nations into a religion of Knowledge, even using scripture and Christian terminology to give to Man what is God's alone.

Oriental philosophies are finding converts in our own public schools and television media. Many are attracted by the disciplined, structured life-style of oriental religions. Through incantations called "mantras," and other devices designed to control Self, the Gnostic way into spiritual enlightenment is once again challenging Christ's Gospel of salvation. The outward guise of discipline, however, cannot substitute for the inner restoration of peace that only the Gospel of the forgiveness of Sin can give, through Jesus Christ.

Chapter 2

E. W. Kenyon:
A Man of His Times

We leave further study of the ancient heresy of Gnosticism to scholars at this point. The Recommended Reading in the final pages will give sources if more comprehensive research material is desired by the reader. As we have seen, there are Gnostic cults in our society today. The Word-Faith movement, however, is the newest and most disguised of all of the Gnostic sects to appear in the last two centuries. It is closer to Christianity than any of the others by reason of its terminology and some of its peripheral doctrines. A word about its originator is necessary at this juncture in tracing the development of Gnosticism into our own times.

Essek W. Kenyon was born in Saratoga County, New York, in 1867. He enrolled as a young man, in the Emerson School of Oratory in Boston, Massachusetts. He seems to have had a conversion experience as a youngster in an evangelistic crusade in New York State. However, he did not choose a seminary, but instead chose a school of Oratory for his college work.

Charles Wesley Emerson, the founder of the Emerson School of the Oratory, is on record at the Mother Church of Christian Science as one of its members from 1903 to 1908, the year of his death. This was very near the time that Kenyon attended the school. The courses offered during Kenyon's studies there included one taught by Dr. Emerson entitled "Bible and Hymn Reading." Perhaps Dr. Emerson's Christian Science training influenced young Kenyon. It is certain that Boston during this era was divided between Christian Science advocates and the Christian churches which were vehemently against their teaching. Whether Kenyon graduated or simply left college to come out West is not clear from the college records. He left and eventually settled in Seattle, Washington to begin pastoring the New Covenant Baptist Church there in about 1937. While pastoring, he broadcast a radio program, "Church of the Air," from 1937 until his death in 1948.

His daughter, Ruth Kenyon Housworth, continues to publish materials from her father's writings and radio recordings. She is president of Kenyon's Gospel Publishing Society in Lynnwood, Washington.

Mrs. Housworth attests to the fact that the only theological training that her father received was through his own study. For an interested reader, as Kenyon certainly was, there was a surge of information pertraining to previous, ancient cultures and Biblical civilizations. Kenyon refers to the "German translators;" his references to the "great, German peoples" seem strangely out of place for one writing during the Second World War.

Whatever the source of his Gnosticism - Christian Science or German-Swiss translators - it is clear that his teachings present perhaps the purest form of Gnosticism that has been seen since the original heresy appeared centuries ago.After Kenyon's death, new teachers used his system to propogate Gnostic ideals. Kenneth Hagin of Tulsa, Oklahoma, began to use Kenyon's teaching; Ken and Gloria Copeland learned Kenyon's system from Hagin, and the Word-Faith teaching became well-known through their radio and television programs. Charles Capps and Jerry Savelle both came out of Copeland's teaching to begin their own, particular emphases: Capps emphasizes the creative powers of the believer and Savelle holds Success Seminars emphasizing financial well-being through the "Word." Oral Roberts University in Tulsa, Oklahoma has become a favorite center for this teaching. Any professor who does not agree with its precepts is endangering his status there at the university. Kenyon's teaching has established roots, flourishing even to the point of becoming a new denomination. This denomination calls itself the "Word Churches." Their various ministries have reached overseas to Europe, South Africa and Australia in a fervor of expansion. In a small village in Mexico, this writer attended a church service during which a woman stood and called her pastors "stupid" for not following the "Word" teachings. She was part-owner of the property on which the church was standing, so the pastors evidently felt it was best not to respond! It is clear that Kenyon's followers are spreading into the whole world with this false gospel.

Word-Faith doctrines, more than other

Gnostic sects like Christian Science or Science of the Mind, are filled with Christian terminology. In fact, one paragraph of orthodox statements might be interjected into paragraphs which deny the Atonement or the Cross of Jesus Christ. The error is less evident when words familiar to the Christian are used from time to time. However, none of these orthodox words become a meaningful part of Kenyon's scheme or system. Rather, they are left like dangling limbs of a tree, not related to the rest of the sturdy, growing organism. These unrelated statements merely serve to confuse the reader and seem to be there to disguise the teaching that has strayed so far from Christianity.

Without an understanding of the tenets of Gnosticism, this System of doctrines cannot be seen for what it is. The overall pattern is lost in a maze of philosophical suggestions without the coordinates of Gnosticism to define where and how the maze is constructed. Let us begin to walk the maze with the Scriptural answers in hand and the light of the Holy Spirit to guide our way.

Chapter 3

Understanding the Word-Faith Doctrines

The first Gnostic concept to be perceived by an observant reader or listener when confronted with the Word-Faith teaching is Dualism. The realm of "Sense Knowledge" is separated from that of "Spiritual Knowledge." Kenyon gives us his concept of reality in the following statement: "The chief quest of Sense Knowledge has been for reality. Man's spirit craves it. Reality cannot be found by [Sense Knowledge]. It is only discovered by the spirit."[1] Sense Knowledge, which refers to the World and the Flesh, is Evil. It is a source of false Knowledge. The believer must ignore this reality and assimilate only that Knowledge coming from spiritual sources - usually only the written scriptures as interpreted by the Word-Faith teachings. This is termed "Revelation Knowledge." Kenyon explains, "Then there is another kind of knowledge that has come to us through the Revelation called the Bible. This is Revelation Knowledge. It brings us in contact with the Creator."[2] Creation cannot be a source of knowledge about its Creator, he asserts. Only a higher Knowledge can lead us to the realm of Deity. Sin and sickness belong in the Evil realm of Sense Knowledge. All of the physical world must be ignored because it only relays false signals from the god of this world, Satan.

The second Gnostic concept that is implied more than stated, is an Unholy Trinity of gods. The three gods include the Creator-God, Man, and Satan. These dignitaries are treated with complete equality, each having their own "legal" rights and privileges, as well as their limitations. Words like, "God couldn't do that; it wasn't legal,'" and our "legal rights" as believers, express this concept of gods operating within the scope of their own, individual limitations. In their Creation story, a mythological re-telling of the Fall of Man, Man fell from divine to satanic. He took the nature of his Father in the beginning, and adopted the nature of his "second" father after the Fall. There is no "human nature" in this tragic tale of lost deity. The phrase, "Man committed 'high treason'," is used to describe Man's fall from equality with God. The Creator-God is unable to help Man because He has already given Man the earth. Man is out of His dominion, in charge of all the Universe. Satan, the "renegade outlaw" of the Universe, is another god. He creates death and darkness. Satan caused Man's Fall and took charge of the earth which had been Man's possession. Like a giant ball, earth was passed from Creator to Man, and finally, to Satan. There is no Sovereign God in this mythology.

The Word-Faith teaching departs on another disastrous course when it introduces the Gnostic concept of Jesus as the "Illuminator," one who shows the Way to others. He is also referred to as the

"Redeemed-Redeemer," by the ancient heretical writers. Like these early heretics, the Word-Faith adherents teach that Jesus, Himself,was in need of redemption at the Cross. He took on the Nature of Satan just like the first Adam did at the Fall. Jesus was Born-Again in the pit of Hell, this teaching asserts, and He became the first of those to be Born-Again into the New Covenant. A Man is seated at the Right Hand of God, not the God-Man, Jesus Christ, of scriptures. The position of Jesus in this system is one of "first among equals." It follows then, that the believer, called the New Creation, is equal with his prototype, Jesus. The believer, too, is given a new, divine nature to replace his former, satanic nature. He is not a sinner-saved-by-grace, but a new "species of being that has never before existed." Through the Knowledge of who the believer "is" in Christ - that is a co-equal with Him - the New Gnostic is in control of his own destiny.

A detailed discussion of the teachings of the Word-Faith movement and their roots in Gnosticism begins with the basis of all of their assertions about themselves, the world, and Reality: the Person of Jesus as Born-Again, the first of all redeemed Mankind.

Chapter 4

The Born-Again Jesus

A Second Fall From Grace

In the Word-Faith teachings, Man was the cause of his own Fall from Grace and he is the source of his own redemption in the person of Jesus. Jesus came as a Man - as perfect as Adam was when God first created him. He is equated by the Word-Faith teachings, with other great men in scripture: "Samuel,...Elijah..the three Hebrew children..all were supermen. ..Jesus was a superman. He lived above natural laws."[1] Jesus is one nature while walking the shores of Galilee and another on the Cross. He is perfect, divinized Man before the Cross, and satanic on the Cross. He is never perceived as fully-God and fully-Man as taught in the scriptures, except for some phrases which carry no weight or consequence to the system of belief.

Just as their mythology changed the story of the first Fall, a myth developed to explain, in Kenyon's teaching, the second Fall: the Fall of Jesus from perfect Man to satanic being in the Garden of Gethsemane. Jesus became obedient to death, scripture states (Phil. 2:8). Kenyon asserts that Satan is the author of Death; by being obedient to death, Jesus thereby became obedient to Satan! Kenyon points out that, "He had been lifted up as a serpent (on the

Cross). Serpent is Satan. Jesus knew He was going to be lifted up, united with the Adversary."[2]

Another scripture from the Old Testament is used to present this teaching that Jesus "died twice," physically and spiritually. In Isaiah 53:9, the verse reads: "His grave was assigned with wicked men, Yet He was with a rich man in His DEATH," (NASB). Kenyon explains this verse by saying, "The word 'death' is plural in the Hebrew, indicating that Jesus died twice on the Cross. He died spiritually [so that]...He could die physically."[3] The word "death" is preceeded by an article, "His." It is true that this article is in the plural in some manuscripts. However, the noun "death" is NOT plural in the Hebrew text. It is also true that the earliest manuscripts do not have the article "His" in the plural. This has led scholars (like Dr. Finley of Talbot Seminary, and others), to assume that the plural article is merely a copyist's error, since it is not accompanied by a plural noun as it should be. Like an elephant balancing on the head of a pin, Kenyon's assumptions about a Born-Again Jesus are balanced on this one article. He and his advocates rest their case on a few manuscripts which have a copyist's error not found in others. If the verse meant "deaths," the word "death" would also be plural in the Hebrew. It is not. The Word-Faith advocates have no excuse to teach a physical and spiritual death of Jesus on the Cross. No translator has ever used the word "deaths" in this verse. A simple error in transcribing occurred, but the meaning of the verse is not changed or compromised in any way.

Substitution and Identification

The Word-Faith teaching's mythological
presentation of the fall of Jesus from
Perfect Man to Satanic denies that
Atonement took place on the Cross. It moves
the redemption of Man to the time after the
supposed double-death of Jesus on the
Cross. As one follower of Kenyon states,
"When [Jesus] said, 'it is finished,' on
that Cross, He was not speaking of the plan
of redemption. The plan of redemption had
just begun. There were still three days
and three nights to go through. ...[In
Hell], He suffered punishment for three
horrible days and nights."[4] They assert
that Jesus was the substitute for every Man
in Hell, and we are identified perfectly
with Him in all aspects of His death and
glory. To tell the story as the Word-Faith
teaching relates it, Jesus did the same
thing that Adam did in the Garden of Eden.
Another advocate of Word-Faith teachings
tells her readers, "He suffered in His own
body, and more important, in His spirit.
Jesus experienced the same spiritual death
that entered Man in the Garden of Eden.
...After Jesus was made sin, He had to be
born again. ...Jesus is a born-again man.
(This is the same new birth that the good
news of the Gospel still offers to any man
who will accept it.)."[5] He accepted the
Sin-Nature of Satan in His own spirit. If
a physical death was the price of Man's
Sin, then any Just Man could have redeemed
Man from Sin, they claim. They assert that
Abel's death could have atoned for Man's
Sin, for example, because "[Abel is] the

first man that died because of honoring
God's word."[6] But, to the Word-Faith mind,
it took the sacrifice of a divinity, the
destruction of Jesus' purity, to open the
Way for Man's restoration to his original,
divine state. There is no cleansing from
Sin in this doctrine, but a complete change
in nature; no atonement but a restoration
of Man to his original status as a god.

Jesus went to Hell like any sinner would,
the myth continues. However, the Father
saw that Jesus had "kept the Law" perfectly
while on earth. Jesus was in Hell
"illegally." Therefore, the Father raised
up Jesus to His Right Hand, re-created His
spirit, and Jesus became the first of many
Born-Again ones. God "looked at the Man on
His Right Hand, and called him 'god,'"
explains one teacher.[7] That's what happened
to you and me, the story continues. It
concludes with the happy ending that every
believer is the hero and heroine. Like the
little books that can be printed with a
particular child's name in the starring
role, the believer is told that the sooner
he forgets Jesus and lives as the center of
the redemption story, the faster that
prosperity and health will come his way.
As this same teacher states, "Unless you've
let Jesus die, you'll never let yourself
live." The believer was identified with
Jesus in every step of this restoration; he
replaces Jesus in his own remembrance of
Calvary and the Throne of God.

Sometimes the myth varies and includes
Knowledge as the tool Jesus used in
overcoming Satan in Hell. This is used by
some teachers to tell their audience that

their Knowledge of the Word of God in scriptures. Whatever the variation, the goal of this foundational teaching is obvious: Man, through Knowledge, can be restored to his divine state. The New Creation is the god who controls his own destiny. These teachings, called "What Happened from the Cross to the Throne," and "Substitution and Identification," are presented on tapes and in books with the same titles. Knowledge is the Way to being like God, and by knowing what happened to Jesus on the Cross, the believer is able to realize his equality with Jesus in all respects.

Chapter 5

The New Creation

The New Creation

The Word-Faith teachings are basically Man-centered, like all Gnostic cults. The main focus, therefore, is upon the believer's identity and powers. The definition of the Born-Again believer rests entirely on the definition of Jesus, the First of those Born-Again. God can do anything in one with faith, like He did in Jesus, their example: "We saw God in Jesus enabling Him to walk the waves of the sea. We saw God in Him multiplying the Bread. Can't you see the possibilities of God in an individual?"[1]

New Creation, their name for the believer, is the same term found in First Corinthians (5:17), but the definition is not at all what scripture teaches about the Christian believer. One evangelist of this teaching repeats Kenyon's words describing the New Creation, "[You are] a new species of being that has never existed before...when you make Jesus your Lord."[2] Another tells us that, "the believer is as much an Incarnation as Jesus Christ."[3] Kenyon's description of New Creation is shrouded with mystery: "A strange day has dawned. The New Creation. It was a 'wonder' day when Jesus was born, but it was a **greater** day when God made provision for the New

Creation!"[4]   His exclamations continue,
"They have the Nature of God...the ability
of God."[5]

Using the Greek word, Zoe (meaning "life"),
they draw its meaning both beyond the scope
of Christian understanding and apart from
scriptural evidence.   This Zoe life is
God's own Nature and Attributes given to
the believer.   One account states that,
"...We have access to His ability, to His
wisdom, to His anointing, to His power, to
His love, and to His faith.   His divine
nature   takes   into   account all   the
attributes of God and we are partakers of
that nature!"[6] This nature melts to become
one with our own desires and will; it will
produce what the believer wants it to: "Any
fruit we have is from our spirit."[7] Once
the person is Born-Again, there is no need
for a god outside of himself. As a god,
the believer can, "...walk as Jesus walked,
without any consciousness of inferiority to
God or Satan, [for] you will have faith
that will stagger the world..."[8]

The Born-Again Christian

The Christian is one who has asked for
forgiveness from Jesus Christ for his Sin,
and believed that Jesus Christ, as revealed
in scripture, is his personal Savior and
Lord of His life. As Lord, He is obeyed,
praised and worshipped above any other
creature that might replace God in his
life.   As the scripture reveals (in Romans
8:16), His Spirit dwells within our spirit:
"The Spirit Himself testifies together with
our own spirit, that we are children of
God."   His Spirit indwells our spirit.

God." His Spirit indwells our spirit.
They are not confused or "fused." The
assurance of being children of God belongs
to those who have been forgiven and washed
in the Blood of the Lamb of God. The
separation between God and the Christian
must be kept as a sacred boundary.
Without this separation, he, himself,
becomes god and center of his destiny.
Like the prodigal son, some want to do what
they will, not what their Heavenly Father
wills. Disaster follows one who refuses
the Lordship of God and listens only to his
desires and wants. It is a subtle form of
idolatry, which is always a serious sin.
The very First Commandment (those
Commandments that Kenyon will not apply to
the New Creation) that God gave to Israel
warned of this. It had serious
consequences in the history of Israel and
will have the same consequences in our own
lives as Christians. More observations
regarding the differences between the Word-
Faith teachings and Christian beliefs are
in the last chapter of this study.

The Day of Pentecost: Birth of New Creations

When Jesus became a New Creation, seated at
the Right Hand of the Father as a mortal
man, he made it possible - in Kenyon's
system - for others to be New Creations,
too. On Pentecost, the apostles and
disciples were given their new, divine
natures. The Gift of Tongues is suitable
speech for a new "species of being."
Kenyon explains," They heard each other
speak in other tongues and their new nature
was speaking."[9] With this as his premise,

Kenyon must somehow prove that not one of Jesus' followers realized that Jesus was their Savior, even after His Resurrection appearances. To keep the system functioning on the New Creation formula, this teaching explains,[10] "When Jesus breathed the Holy Spirit upon the Apostles [after His Resurrection], this was so that they could momentarily have the 'inspiration' to understand His teaching." While on earth, before He was a New Creation, Jesus could not save anyone. Kenyon says that, "[Jesus] could not give anyone Eternal Life because it was not available until after He had [been exalted]."[11] Zoe life was only available to others when Jesus was exalted as the first New Creation.

Power Plays

The search for power apart from the Person of the indwelling Holy Spirit - in those who are Christian by virtue of their acceptance of Jesus Christ as personal Savior - is clearly seen in the original Gnostic, Simon the Magician. He desired power (Acts 8:9-24) from the Apostles and was willing to pay money for the power of the Holy Spirit. Simon outwardly appeared to accept the Good News of salvation in Christ and was baptized in water. However, when the Apostles came up from Jerusalem and were ministering the Holy Spirit, Simon said to them, "Give this authority to me..". Even after Simon's baptism, his heart had not changed, and Peter said to him,"I see that you are in the gall of bitterness and in the bondage of iniquity." Evidently, Peter's warning to repent of his own search for power that caused him to combine Greek and oriental mythology with the Gospel of Grace.

Kenyon describes his search for power:"How well I remember the years I sought for power with God, prayed for power, and read every book I could find that would tell me how to get it."[12] However, with power safe in the hands of God, the Christian is assured that the Love of God will define His use of that power in our own lives.

Chapter 6

The Word-Faith Covenant

The basis of the Word-Faith Covenant's operation is Knowledge. Knowledge of the spiritual laws is necessary, as is Knowledge of the believer's rights and privileges under his covenant. As one teacher, Charles Capps, tells his readers, "You can have what you say. ...Through the Knowledge of God." Capps quotes scripture (II Peter 1:3) "according as his divine power hath given unto us all things..through the knowledge of him that hath called us to glory and virtue." Capps seeks to prove that by having God's own Knowledge, the believer can have all that he speaks: "His divine power has given unto us all things - all things- how? through the Knowledge of God. He is saying that if you get the knowledge of God, then you have the wisdom of God; and the wisdom of God is the Word of God."[1] This teaching is claiming for its followers a share in the very Knowledge of God - that Knowledge that He possesses as Sovereign God over all. This Knowledge gives the believer power to claim anything that he wishes to obtain. The summation of this Knowledge is the (written) Word of God. By using the written Word of God, this power is activated. Kenyon remarks that, "A strong confession coupled with a corresponding action on the Word brings God on the scene."[2] God, the force for Good, does what the believer has commanded Him to do with His own Word. In the Word-Faith concept of Knowledge, God waits upon the words of the Word-Faith believer. The Word of God in the Bible is God's "spiritual law," and as a law it must be kept at all costs. Grace is not necessary for the Word-Faith believer, for God's Grace is replaced by the Law. These spiritual laws are only those scripture verses that are singled out as law by the Word-Faith teachers. Verses that contradict their assumptions are given another interpretation or ignored altogether. As in any Law-based religion, the responsibility lies on the believer for success or failure. Success is measured by the degree of prosperity and health enjoyed by the Word-Faith adherent. The pharisees of Jesus' time would find close friends among the Faith teachers. Those who are chronically ill or in financial difficulties are urged to "have faith and confess results." The scriptural command to "Love one another," is ignored, and it's every man for himself in this cold-hearted view of spiritual laws. This New Covenant has nothing to do with the Old Covenant described in the Old Testament, they contend. The Old Testament is written by those with lesser Knowledge than Pauline Revelation.

The Exchange System

Kenyonites need only confess with the mouth that Jesus is Lord. The words provide for an exchange of lords. Confession replaces prayer in the believer's life, they believe. He need not ask for forgiveness of sin nor does he need to repent in the

Word-Faith system. Instead of believing, as Christians do, in the Atonement of Christ for Sin, and in coming to Christ for forgiveness, the Atonement is denied. Forgiveness is unnecessary, since Sin is taken care of, in Kenyon's system, by the exchange of Lords (from Satan to Christ) and the exchange of Natures (from satanic to divine). He says that "if it were possible for God to forgive a sinner his sins, it would do no good, because the sinner would go on sinning.."[3] The sinner would remain unchanged, he asserts; Man has had no change in his sinful Nature. Man, instead, must be reconciled to his former position as god of the Universe - reconciled to the state that Adam was in from the beginning of Creation. Jesus, then, becomes a pattern, the first of a new race, and not a Redeemer or Savior from Sin. The Word-Faith Jesus, whom they claim as lord, is a diabolical substitute that exists only in the minds of men who desire to be like God, Himself. This teaching ignores the entire Old Testament preparation for the physical sacrifice of the Lamb of God, "without blemish," who would die for the sins of all. Instead, they compile a New Covenant, constructed to their own specifications, which is unrelated to any other Covenant in the Old Testament. It is without the testimony of God.

The Christian Response

Let's pause for a moment, and consider what Christians really DO believe. The comparison will be all the more clear when it is presented face-to-face with the Word-

47

Faith teaching. Christians know from scripture that God is a holy God. Sin not only caused Man to need forgiveness, but required propitiation - that is, a satisfaction of the requirements of a Holy God. The sacrifice of Christ has satisfied God's wrath against Sin due to the demands of His Holiness (I Jn. 2:2). Contrary to Kenyon's thesis, the word "Atonement" is found in the New Testament. The Hebrew word is "kippur"; it is translated "reconciliation." Grace is now available through Calvary, to conform us continually to the Holiness of God, not just to initially reconcile us to God. Through Christ's work of propitiation in His sacrifice on Calvary - that is, His **physical** death on the Cross - He satisfied the full penalty for Sin that God required. God can now justly forgive the sins of those who come to Him through the Blood of Christ. The "life is in the Blood," as the Book of Leviticus proclaims, and when the Christian asks to be cleansed by the Blood of Christ, it is the very Life of Christ that covers and cleanses the one Born-Again into newness of Life. Our nature is not changed but it is completed. A human spirit is reborn within the life of the new Christian. Kenyon's desire for a divine Nature has no place in the scriptural teaching that Christians share and partake in the fellowship with the Father. We are covered with the Righteousness of Christ. Kenyon has desired equality with God, not dependence upon Him for Grace and continuing mercy. Man must do his part to appropriate God's redemption available through Christ. It is not the mere speaking forth with the mouth, but a repent heart that asks Christ for forgiveness of his sins. Man is reconciled with God when he turns to Jesus Christ, God's Way to Salvation. By virtue of the two Natures of Jesus Christ - Divine and Human- He was able to both satisfy a Holy God and reconcile Mankind with his Creator. In Isaiah (Chapter 53) and in I Peter (2:24), the scripture specifically states that the Redeemer-Christ bore our Sin on HIS BODY OF FLESH. The Word-Faith teaching insists that Christ's suffering was in His Spirit, destroying His Divine Nature. Scripture tells us that Christ committed His Spirit to the Father on the Cross. Surely, Kenyon cannot accuse the Lord, Himself, of lying? The stripes upon His back were spiritual and physical healing for those who would trust in His salvation. Physical healing refers to the Resurrection of the Saints, and makes physical healing possible within God's Will for each. Old Testament sacrifices were intricate in detailing various treatments of the flesh of animals to be sacrificed. Jesus' Sacrifice on Calvary fulfilled each and every sacrifice typified in the Old Testament, thereby fulfilling (not eradicating) the Old Covenant. God is Immutable, Unchanging - His Word is continuous through the Old and New Testaments. His plan of Salvation has not varied from one century to another. He is faithful to fulfill and complete His wonderful Design for His People. Kenyon and his followers have refused the Gospel of Jesus Christ's Atonement and have replaced it with a devilish concept of a Jesus who went to Hell, like any sinner, and needed to be Born-Again. It is not astonishing that others teach a false gospel, for this has happened from the inception of Christianity. What is astonishing is that the Christian church, the Charismatic community in particular, has been so willing to accept this obvious departure from the Cross of Jesus Christ. We have been asleep while the Enemy has infiltrated the very sanctuary of the Church.

The Blood in the Word-Faith Covenant

The Blood of Jesus, as one might guess having read other doctrines of Kenyon, takes on an entirely new character not found in scripture. Kenyon will proclaim that, "The Blood Covenant was the basis on which the New Covenant was founded."[4] The Blood of Christ, like Christ, Himself, is reduced to a symbol of equality between Jesus and the New Creation believer. Kenyon explains, "When Abraham cut the covenant, they (he and God) became one.. 'I am the Vine and ye are the branches'."[5] He uses the example of the cutting of the covenant between blood-brothers common to many cultures and tribes. Kenyon regards the Last Supper as a celebration of a common bond of fellowship. As Copeland's words indicate, the Blood simply ratifies the Covenant made between Jesus and those who follow after Him, "Jesus also said, 'This is My blood that ratifies the covenant. Drink of My blood and as often as you drink it, do it in remembrance of Me.' ..I want you to remember the covenant that He has made available to you - the power that He has made yours."[6] The Gospel of Matthew, which is almost always found in Communion services, has been replaced by another. The usual Christian service includes the verse, "This is My Blood which is poured out for many for the forgiveness of sins,"(Matt. 26:28). Without a Blood-Atonement, Kenyon's Gospel has clearly aligned itself with other Gnostic cults denying the Atoning Blood of Jesus Christ.

Wealth and Health in the Word-Faith Covenant

Every part of the Word-Faith Covenant is dependent on the "Faith" of the believer. However, the meaning assigned to "Faith" is directly opposed to the definition of Faith found in the scriptures. Biblical Faith is that of complete trust in God's Will, not necessarily seeing the results of that trust. Examples of this kind of Faith are given in the Book of Hebrews (Chapter Eleven). After naming men and women of faith, the description continues (verse 39), "..And all of these, though they won divine approval by their faith, did not receive the fulfillment of what was promised..;" these faithful did not see the fulfillment of what they were trusting God for, but perservered in Faith to the end. As the first verse of the chapter reads, "Faith is the assurance of things hoped for, being the proof of things (we) do not see --faith perceiving as real fact what is not revealed to the senses," (Amplified Version). Faith, itself, substitutes for sight; nothing else is needed for the person who has real trust in God. However, Kenyon's gospel requires that Faith produce what is desired; the believer must bring about, through Faith, whatever he has desired so that it may be seen and felt now. This is Faith in "faith," or even "faith in words," but it is not Faith that rests on and relies on God for the outcome. The Faith of the Word-Faith teaching is really that of the old adage, Seeing is Believing. Kenyon states, "When prayer (confession) does not produce miracles it is but empty words...a miracle is God moving in the sense realm. "[7] The following story, told by Ken Hagin, shows that outward prosperity is a measure of faith. Lack of results always means disaster for the believer: "..a business deal fell through - the man was out of the Will of God. He had had a palatial home...and he lost it."[8] Yet, the Christian knows that prosperity can lead him out of God's Will as surely as it can benefit him. God does provide for His children;, but praying for wealth and riches is a signal that the love of money has taken root, no matter how the words seek to disguise the motive. One assistant pastor of a church teaching this doctrine, was heard to begin his prayer for prosperity by addressing Wealth: "O wealth," he said, "we call upon you.. ." No doubt, he meant to have the forces of wealth put into motion, but God was certainly not the Object of the prayer. Copeland interprets the Gospel story of the Rich Young Man in the light of Word-Faith definitions: "..Jesus ..said..(that) what he lacked was a working revelation of the Covenant. ...He walked off sadly because he had great possessions. ...If the man had really known the Covenant, he would have thought, 'what does the Covenant say about giving to the poor?' This was the biggest **financial** deal that young man had ever been offered, but he walked away from it because he didn't know God's system of finance.

...He assumed that God wanted to break him."[9]   The Rich Young Man could have become "richer" following Jesus, according to their interpretation. Any reference to the Cross is excused as a cross of bearing with others; it never includes suffering of any kind. Such interpretations are so far removed from the Gospel of Jesus Christ that they hardly need comment. Yet, these teachings are being received by Christians without a murmur, in most cases. If there is criticism, the Word-Faith adherents claim persecution because of their superior Knowledge.   They are different, they contend, and because of this, others are threatened.   Like the Stranger, Allogenes, of Ancient Gnosticism, these elitists feel that they are above the common Christian. Copeland tells his followers that even Jesus felt alone and persecuted. Referring to the words of Jesus that :"the Son of Man has nowhere to lay His Head," he explains that Jesus was describing His Loneliness. Like all New Creations, they postulate, Jesus was above the common crowd of sinful men. Not because He was fully God and fully Man, but because He had higher Knowledge of the Word of God.

Chapter 7

Weapons of Warfare

The Lord Jesus spoke to all Christians when He commanded them not to go into the world with the message of His redemption until they were baptized in the Holy Spirit. Whether all Christians use this terminology or not, all would agree that without the power of God's Spirit in their lives, the path of service in Christ to the church and to the world is a difficult, if not impossible one. But, the Christian who has humbled himself, and called upon Jesus Christ for this Gift of His Spirit, knows the wonderful Presence of God in a special way. The Christian who has been filled with the Holy Spirit, and walks in this Spirit, has the One Who defeats Satan in every battle. By listening to the Holy Spirit, Christians are guided and directed into their own, individual part in the conflict. Faith and trust in God sustain all of us in times of direct, spiritual warfare with the Enemy of our souls. To refuse evidence of spiritual conflict, or evidence of any supernatural event in individual lives, is to marry blindness and confusion. Some Christians want to walk as natural men, when the Scriptures tell us that principalities and powers are in conflict with the children of God. The road to walking in the Spirit is the road of humble waiting upon Him to fill us with Himself, and then to guide us in His Way. He is all the Power that Christians need; He is All in all. However, Word-Faith followers do not want God, but only His Power and authority to do as they please. In order to claim His power as their own, they must divide the Person of God into various parts, so that they may have power piece by piece.

Name of Jesus

Kenyon's New Creation believer has three weapons available to him for warring against the god of this world and any evil circumstance. According to the Word-Faith teaching, the Name of Jesus, the written Word of God, and confession aloud of desired results all release the forces of Good for the believer. The Name of Jesus is carefully divorced from the Person of the Lord Jesus. As in the ancient form of this heresy, separations between various attributes and the Person of the Godhead allow for an impersonal use of these qualities without reference to the living God. For example, the Name of Jesus is seen to be the greatest "gift" of Jesus to the Apostles at Pentecost: "What a strange hush must have come upon the hearts of the disciples when they realized..that that Name was the center around which everything revolved! ...in that Name - the Name of their absent Lord - all the work of the early Church was wrought."[1] There was no necessity for Jesus, Himself; His Name replaced His power in the lives of the apostles and disciples. It was given to anyone who did what Jesus did - who was Born-Again like He was, they conclude. The first recipient of this powerful Name was,

of course, the first of the New Creations -
Jesus: "..We have seen that the Father
has lifted Him to the highest position in
the universe.   He has conferred upon Him
the highest Name in the Universe...and this
Name is given to us." ² One is never to
pray to Jesus, but only to the Father in
the Name of Jesus. This assertion strips
Jesus Christ of His equality with the
Father. The Holy Spirit is also lost in
the array of weapons that the Nature of the
New Creation has in himself.

To the New Gnostics of the Word-Faith
teaching, God has left the earth in the
hands of re-born Man. He has given to Man
the weapons necessary to become conquerors
of the earth again, wresting it from the
hands of Satan. Knowledge is the key to
the use of these weapons of the Name of
Jesus and confession of the written
scriptures: "The moment a man knows that he
has a legal right to stand in the Father's
presence, just as freely as Jesus, that
moment Satan's dominion over him ends?"
Using the Name sets the believer apart from
the rest of Mankind.   Kenyon   insists
that,"The New Creation must learn the
secret and Joy and blessing of using the
Name of Jesus as you would use a wrench to
tighten a nut on a bolt, as you would use a
knife to cut a piece of meat." ⁴   This Name
is clearly devoid of any link with the
living Jesus Christ.   It is merely an
impersonal tool to be used at the whim of
the New Creation. The power to use this
Name was given at Pentecost: "...The
[apostles] made a discovery - the Name of
the Man Whom they had loved, whom they had
seen nailed to that cross...now has power

equal to the power that He, Himself, exercised when He was among them."[5] Jesus used His Name first, they teach, and the New Creation may use it as freely as He did with the same results. Yet, there are instances in the Gospels that disciples failed. This was because, Kenyon reasons, "They were Jews under the First Covenant, with unregenerated spirits. You cannot find any folly as that in the Pauline Revelation."[6] Kenyon places Pauline Revelation above the Gospels. The latter were written under the Old Covenant; the Pauline Epistles were written to reveal the whole of the New Covenant.

The Written Word of God

The higher revelation of Paul, according to Kenyon, was written for the New Covenant men. Word-Faith teachings rely on Paul's Epistles almost to the exclusion of other scriptures. They believe that the Bible is a "god" unto itself, needing only the power of the New Creation's tongue to put its force into action. Speaking, called confession, becomes all that is necessary to control the circumstances surrounding the believer. Kenyon explains:" When we realize [that scripture replaces Christ], we have discovered the key that even the disciples and apostles did not have." Again, Kenyon declares that, "The written word was not known to them [the apostles] except in a very limited way."[8] In fact, while claiming to be teaching the uncompromised Word of God, Word-Faith teachers dismiss some scriptures as being without the anointing of the Holy Spirit. Since the early biblical figures did not have the written Word, they could not have the same Knowledge that the New Creation believer has. Capps explains this point of view: "Job did say ["The Lord gave, and the Lord hath taken away;.."] it, but it is not a true statement. It is a lie. Did you know there are lies recorded in the Bible?...Job sure was not under the anointing when he made that statement. He could not <u>read</u> chapter 1 of the book of Job. So he had an excuse for saying what he did. ..[But] it was satan that took away everything Job had."[9] When scripture does not agree with the Word-Faith teachings, the Word of God is changed to fit the ideas of these men. Their claim to be teaching the Word of God is a distortion of fact, one perhaps designed to discourage any investigation of their real stand concerning the Word of God. An example of their continual reference to the "Word" instead of Jesus Christ, is the change of the familiar scripture to read, "It is the WORD in your heart that makes you free." By replacing Jesus with the written Word in all scripture references, they ignore any personal relationship with Jesus in favor of simply reading and memorizing certain scripture verses.

Confessing Results

Confession replaces prayer because prayer only causes the believer to repeat the problem, continuing to give the evil forces energy to operate. The Word-Faith teachings must ignore, therefore, all the scriptural admonitions to pray, and replace prayer with their own term, Confession. Jesus, Himself, they teach, confessed Who He was,

thereby rising to the level of a true Man
of Faith. Kenyon proclaims, "[Jesus said]
I am the Way, Truth and the Life..What a
confession! ...Christianity is the Way..We
point to the Way."[10] Any praying merely
puts the believer in the Sense Realm of
unbelief, as Kenyon states that, " I used
to consecrate and surrender to the Lord
daily. I found out after a while I was
running in a circle. ...Our redemption is
in the past tense."[11] Confession involves
demanding that Satan release the world's
goods or wealth to the believer, the new
god of this world: "Satan can do in your
life what you will allow him to do. As
long as you pray, Satan will 'operate.'
This is not the time to pray! God didn't
let that thing happen to you - you did."[12]
Confession usually relies on a verse from
scripture, coupled with a command which is
tagged with the Name of Jesus at the end.
Because they insist that any use of the
Word of God must always create what is
spoken, results must always be forthcoming.
They have relegated the Will of God to a
few verses containing promises in agreement
with the Word-Faith teaching, instead of
encompassing all of God's designs for His
Beloved. By using only a few verses, they
limit God's actions to those things chosen
by the believer to be desirable. God is
servant to the believer. But, they claim,
Jesus used these principles and so must
everyone who is Born-Again: "Jesus
'operated' in faith principles...He
operated in the God-kind of Faith."[13] With
the weapon of Confession, the believer can
rely on his own ability for all good: "[The
New Creation] becomes God's 'agent,' giving
men Eternal Life, making them masters."[14]

all He's going to do, the Word-Faith teachers claim, and it is up to the New Creation believers to win the battles using their abilities and faith. Hope is scorned in this context: "If you are going to get your heart's desire in the future, it will never materialize."[15] Word-Faithers would say that Faith is the "substance of things SEEN," not of things unseen, as the Book of Hebrews clearly states. However, Word-Faith Confession never takes "No" for an answer, even when that "no" comes from God, Himself. Any failures to receive, or see, the results of the believer's Confession is blamed on the faith of the believer. One teacher sternly reminds his reader that, "It is easier to blame God than to admit that we failed to act on the (written) Word."[16] Another states that, "If you pray according to God's (written) Word and follow Instructions, you will get results. If you miss it, then its your faith at fault."[17] Their mentor, Kenyon, is quick to place the blame on the believer: "You are suffering...because you have refused your place in Christ."[18] Ignorance is the worst sin in the books of the Word-Faith teaching. The believer is blamed because the fruits of the Spirit are really the fruits of his own spirit. As Kenyon tells his followers, "Faith is product of your spirit, just as wisdom is a product of your spirit; faith is developedaand wisdom is enriched by meditation in the Word of God."[19] A typical Word-Faith "prayer" is not a prayer, but an affirmation, or Confession, of what is desired. In Hagin's devotional booklet, Faith Food, affirmations are printed out for the reader. The Confession for January First reads: "In this upcoming year my faith will grow. I am determined my knowledge of God's Word will grow. My understanding of God's Word will grow. Therefore faith will come. My faith will grow. I will grow and develop spiritually this year." With this heavy burden of confession (and condemnation if results fail to materialize), the one who wishes to follow the Word-Faith teachings is in danger of sinking into a pit of self-deprecation and estrangement from God. God's Will flows from His Love for the Christian. The will and words of men cannot bring life or goodness, but will only bring a sense of failure and loss.

Chapter 8

Problems of Sin and Sickness

A Christian who periodically watches religous television described a televised Word-Faith Convention. The instructions to those in wheel chairs - which included the entire front row in a large arena - was to rise, if their faith was strong enough, and walk. The havoc that followed was soul-wrenching to this viewer. Some persons struggled in obedience to the command, and fell in front of their chairs. From there, they were literally crawling, moving their bodies as best they could along on the floor, straining to get up. The response of those in charge, however, seemed to be one of unconcern. No move was made, that was visible to the television audience, to pray or instruct them. This appearance of cold and aloof behavior would seem to indicate an unusual attitude toward sickness which is part of the Word-Faith teaching. It would insist that it is up to the believer to have the faith to get well. In a strange sort of competition, it's every man for himself in the "faith walk." Only the strong survive, some would say. This seems to be a gospel of fear in which the weak may be despised as failures; it is not the Gospel of Jesus Christ which reaches out in love to others. Their teaching is a stranger to love of God or the brethren. The measurements of health and wealth are necessary to Word-Faithers because signs of success in faith are all

EXternal. This is especially true of the
teachers, themselves. They, more than any
others, are expected to bear external
"fruits" of their confession. They are the
experts who never need hospital care or
financial aid. If money is not flowing
into bank accounts, or if a cold or flu has
found its way into the family, immediate
accusations come from others in this
teaching. God's Word always works, they
say. As Gloria Copeland instructs, "To
prosper in the faith walk, you must first
make a decision that God's Word does not
fail. If the Word of God does not seem to
be working for you, it is not God's fault.
There is something you don't know. More
than likely, you are just not standing
firm."[1] Failure is never admitted or
allowed. They confess to others that
everything is just fine, and deny the
reality that is surrounding them. Prayer
and fellowship with the Father is rarely
discussed. Their battle with the Enemy is
all-consuming; the struggle is continuous
against his attacks. Indoctrination into
Word-Faith doctrines is subtle and slow,
replacing scripture study and prayer with
tapes and books by these teachers. Mental
health deteriorates along with spiritual
health. The reality presented by the world
of our senses which keep us in touch with
our surroundings must be denied. The view
that Satan is the giver of Evil, and that
Sin is only the product of an imaginary
mind, takes its toll on the mental health
of the believer trying to do the
impossible. This denial of reality begins
with the concept of the New Creation as a
perfect being - incapable of sinning.

The Mirage of Sin

Sin is treated like a mirage of the Sense World, in Word-Faith. They ignore it as one would ignore any figment of the imagination. Sin is not Reality for the New Creation; the Word-Faith teachers claim an exchange of Natures at the point of new birth. With their share of God's own Nature, sin becomes impossible. Kenneth Hagin has said, "Sin is only what I think. There is a higher Knowledge of what God says [about the New Creation], that is always right."[2] Therefore, any sense of sin is really Satan telling the believer lie, they say. This teaching contends that believers must sense no inferiority because of sinfulness which does not exist: "When you learn to walk as Jesus walked, without any consciousness of inferiority to God or Satan, you have faith that will stagger the world... ."[3] True Knowledge, using Word-Faith terms, is higher than the awareness of sin or sickness. These only come from Sense Knowledge, as Kenyon explains, "The word for Knowledge in greek is 'epignosis,' it means full Knowledge, exact Knowledge, for it is [contained]; in this Revelation [Pauline Epistles]."[4] With this fullness of Knowledge, the Word-Faith follower claims to know better than to believe in Sin or Sickness. However, Kenyon fails to note that the word for Knowledge can be one of two words, Gnosis or Epignosis. The latter refers to Knowledge which comes through the living out or experience of a truth in life. Gnosis is a more general term for knowledge. Epignosis does not imply a higher -that is a different and better- revelation from God. The whole Word of God

65

is the best revelation because it all comes from Him.   Kenyon, however, insists that Christianity is not "patching up damaged goods," but an exchange of a bad nature for a perfect one. He says, "Christianity is..not having your sins forgiven.   It   is receiving the Nature of God, Eternal Life [Zoe]."[5] Zoe, as we have mentioned, is interpreted in Word-Faith terms to mean God's own Nature with all of His Attributes of perfection. These become the believer's own abilities, they would say.   Therefore, Sin is only a product of the mind.

Word-Faith teachings often use Deuteronomy (Chapter 28) as a provision for healing from sickness.   "Christ has redeemed us from the curse of the Law," Hagin writes, "...The Bible says that all sickness and disease is a curse of the law."   To   claim the blessings of following the Law, and yet refuse the curses which were attached to breaking the Law, is inconsistant at the very least. More than that, it is a denial of the New Covenant of Grace. Since Christians are not under the Law, neither its blessings nor curses would apply to them. The verse in Galatians (3:13) states that Christ has redeemed the Christian from following the Law at all! The New Covenant is a continuation o the Abrahamic Covenant. The Law was a burden, given to show Man's sinfulness in bold relief against God's Holiness. The Blessing of Abraham is the Promise of the Holy Spirit,Who would indwell each believer through the Messiah (Gal.3:14).   The Prophet, Ezechial, looked forward to the New Covenant of God's own Spirit dwelling within each faithful one, and the personal obedience that   would follow. Christians inherit the promises of Abrahamic Covenant, not the Covenant of Mount Sinai. The weight of Sin and the Law has been lifted through the Blood of Jesus Christ in forgiveness and repentance. It is through the confession of sins that the Christian walks in continuing Grace and mercy from God. In spite of Word-Faith claims to the contrary, Christianity is the forgiveness of sins, and a sharing in God's wonderful Grace. The difference between God and His creatures is as vast as His Infinity. It has been bridged by the Incarnate Son of God, Jesus Christ. But those who are blinded by a doctrine that struts its successes and hides its failures, are rebellious children who refuse to depend upon God or His Son for anything.

The Mirage of Sickness

Sickness is the result of some failure to obey God's Word, say Word-Faith teachers. It is a mirage that should not be believed, nor should it be acted on in any way. Satan is the author of sickness, and it is up to the believer to deny it and bring about healing with this denial. This Word-Faith supposition has grown out of an assumption in the Pentecostal and Charismatic communities that healing is provided for in the Atonement. However, Jesus Christ atoned for Sin, redeeming our souls, but the fullness of redemption for our bodies is not yet in our times. At the resurrection of the Saints, the human body will experience the fullness of redemption, just as the soul's redemption is assured by the Cross of Calvary even now. In Eternity, everything is accomplished in

Christ, but in the element of Time, all has not yet been completed in Redemption History. For example, prophecies of Israel's return as a nation went unfulfilled for centuries. Biblical prophecy is the eternal point of view, spoken by God to assure the faithful that His plan is working for them; human history is waiting for certain provisions of Christ's Redemption to be available in Time. THIS IS NOT TO SAY THAT PHYSICAL HEALING IS NOT AVAILABLE TO THE CHRISTIAN! Not at all! Sickness, like any circumstance that comes to the Christian, is an individual matter to be taken to the Lord in prayer with faith. Each case is unique, but Jesus always has the answer, even as He did while on earth. Sometimes, the answer will be a doctor, and at other times, it will be necessary to rebuke the Enemy. The Holy Spirit will give each Christian the specific answer intended by the Lord to be carried out by His own. To substitute a formula of certain, magical words, or to always come against the Enemy without discernment, is to introduce a system of Law that always "works." In continually rebuking the Enemy, the believer implies that the Enemy is the only one with which he has to deal. Christians must search out God's Will, for he is God's child. The Holy Spirit knows the depths of God, and searches out our own hearts, according to scripture. He is the still, small Voice to Whom the Christian listens for specific answers to sickness.

The belief that healing is always and everywhere immediately available according to the amount of faith in the individual,

has followed from the insistence that
healing is provided for in the Atonement.
Sin and Sickness are given the same
dimensions and provisions in time for the
believer, by Word-Faith teachings. Healing
becomes, therefore, just as important as
salvation in the minds of these believers.
Using the Word of God like a magical book
of recipes for success in healing, they
claim results every time, in the same way.
Healing has become, along with wealth, a
sign of the amount of faith in the
believer. Most, if not all, Word-Faith
teachers will never admit to having been
sick. Never mind their gall-bladder
operations or broken legs that are known to
a few followers; admission of the necessity
of hospitalization is tantamount to
admission to a lack of faith on their part.
Mrs. Copeland writes that, "If you put the
Word of God in your heart, act on it, and
obey it, you will always get healed."[6] She
continues, "Begin to think like God thinks
and act like God acts."[7] This is a heavy
assignment for a mere human being! But she
is talking to New Creation believers who
think that they are equal with God. Any
scripture which mentions "God," is assigned
a new meaning. She quotes Isaiah 26:3:
"'Thou wilt keep him in perfect peace whose
mind is stayed upon Thee..' When you spend
your time in the Word, and stay your mind
on the Word, you will be kept in perfect
peace.. ."[8] She smoothly changes the
reference to God into keeping our minds on
"the Word." This "Word" only refers to
those verses which are in agreement with or
changeable enough to fit into Word-Faith
doctrine. Believers share God's power for
Good, as Kenneth Hagin changes another

verse from John 14:14,   "If you ask Me anything in My Name, I will do it." Hagin says that, "Here, the Greek word translated 'ask' means 'demand.' ..Let that soak in a little.   You're not demanding anything of the Father..You're demanding of the Devil.⁹" However, the Greek word used in that verse is "AITEO."   Another Greek word means "demand: "EROTEO." In this verse, Jesus said to His disciples, "Ask of **Me**.. ," not "ask of Satan." If Word-Faithers confuse their concept of Jesus with Satan, they are justified in doing so.

The problem that the Word-Faithers have concerning Evil in the World is the same as that of most unbelievers who question the Christian.   How can a loving God permit Evil?   Nations rise against nations, neighbors against neighbors in our own sphere of activity, and evil stalks the land.   Unbelievers try to make God into Man's Image, reasoning that a good man could not allow Evil to go on, therefore, why should a Good God? Their false concept of God is one with dimensions infinitely smaller than God's true Nature. His Nature is Love.   Not Love as Man understands it, but real Love. The Bible describes God as dwelling in "unapproachable Light," and as a "Consuming Fire;" these express His Glorious Presence and Holiness. Love is nested, in Him, with His Holiness and Justice. This is certainly not present in unsanctified, human "love." Jesus Christ, His Incarnation on earth, showed us that God's greatest desire is that all be saved from Hell and eternal punishment. He will use strong means to that end, to save those who have refused to obey Him.   If His

methods seem harsh, perhaps it is that we
have not loved as He has; perhaps we do not
realize the consequences of our refusal of
Him as He knows them to be? His love knows
no bounds - the heights and depths of His
love are without limit - and this love has
sought out Mankind from the very beginning.
As Paul cries out, "Oh, the depth of the
riches both of the wisdom and knowledge of
God! How unsearchable are His judgments
and unfathomable His ways!" (Rom. 11:33,
NASB).

Yet, the Word-Faith teachings cannot abide
having another god in control of their
lives. It cannot trust another with its
salvation. As Mrs. Copeland indicates, in
a phrase right out the mouth of unbelief,
"How can you say that a loving God would
put sickness on you.. ."10 And again, "As a
believer, you are in authority in the earth
over Satan and sickness and disease."11 She
replaces God with the believer. This is
what the Holy Spirit speaks to our church
today: "For if one comes and preaches
another Jesus whom we have not
preached...Such men are false apostles.."
(II Cor.11:4,13-15,NASB).

Chapter 9

Forces of Good and Evil

Gnosticism has a dualistic concept of the world, as already discussed in Ancient Gnosticism. This dualism extends into the Nature of Man, himself. Man is not a synthesis of soul and body, or even spirit, soul and body, but he is simply "spirit." The body is a non-essential part of Man's being, the vessel whereby his spirit can move and act. The spirit of Man is the Real Man. The physical matter is unreal in the sense that it is to be ignored as a part of this earth and its material unreality. Because scripture affirms that Man made in the "image of God," Kenyon bolts to the conclusion that Man is "God's Class of Being." Man is Spirit, and so is God, he concludes. There were no differences between them in Nature at the beginning. When Sin came into the picture, Man's Nature changed from God's to Satan's. The problem was in his spirit, which is his only real Nature. Therefore, Kenyon asserts, redemption must have taken place in the spiritual realm, not the physical. Jesus must have suffered the consequences of Sin in His Spirit, not in His Flesh. The misunderstanding goes back to the beginning of Man in Creation and the problem of Sin. One who has read Genesis knows that God continues to deal with Adam, covering him with skins. Adam and Eve still commune with God; He still directs their ways. They do not become Satanic, although Sin takes its toll in physical death and a curse upon the Earth. Man was not cursed by God; the earth was cursed and Man was required to expend the sweat of his brow to toil and reap a harvest. According to Kenyon's gospel, however, Man was cursed and became satanic with a new father, Satan. As Gloria Copeland says, "{Adam} lived under the dominion of Satan whose nature is spiritual death. By his own free will Adam subjected himself and his kingdom to Satan. ...Every phase of Adam's life came under the curse of his new god, Satan."[1] God is still God, however, and this misinterpretation is not in the scriptural account at all. Sinful ways without repentance did cause many of those before the Flood to walk in terrible rebellion against God so that God destroyed them. He led Noah and his family because they continued to be faithful to Him. There is no reason to believe that God threw Mankind away to another god, Satan. This is the result of Word-Faither's wishful thinking; they wish that God would be out of their way so that Man and Satan would be gods equal to the One God. Rebellious hearts do not want to be subject to Almighty God and His Will!

The physical world is within the entire scope of redemption; God has not given up on His Creation. Jesus Christ suffered physically, bearing our Sins upon His Body of Flesh, and He physically resurrected. His Resurrection is a sign of our own physical resurrection, and that earth and its creatures will be redeemed out of Sin and death at that time. To place the action of redemption within the spirit only is to deny the reality of the flesh or the goodness of the material creation. This is, of course, exactly what Gnosticism in all of its forms does deny. The object of Gnostic thought is to gain freedom for Man from both God and Satan, from both Good and Evil. To do this, he must be aware of the Forces of both in order to manipulate them for his desires.

In the mind of the Word-Faith believer, he is alone with certain verses of scripture and his own redeemed nature in the battle against Satan and his evil conjurings of Sin and Sickness. Victory depends on his Knowledge (Gnosis) of these forces which are at work. The words of his mouth activate these forces for Good or Evil. The believer must never say words like "I nearly died laughing," or "it killed me." These words carry power in and of themselves to bring about what believers speak, no matter what the intent in speaking. The mental gymnastics required to screen any damaging words out of conversations or even thought are exhausting. These Forces put in operation are impersonal "gods" with names like Patience, Faith, Righteousness, Fear and many others. They perform what their names signify. Words of Faith create the Force of Faith, and so on. As Charles Capps writes, "The principles of faith are based on spiritual law...you set them in motion by words of your mouth That's the way you are saved, by confessing Jesus as Lord. ...Faith-filled words released [by you]...defeated Satan and created the reality of God's Word in your spirit.[2]"

This Gnostic world of inner and outer forces relegates the Living God to biblical history. God is not an ever-present Lord Who forgives sins, but He has given Man the tools for his own salvation, His Word. Capps describes Pentecost when the Apostles received their New Natures: "They were not now sinners saved by grace, but new creations in Christ...Natural men became supernatural men. New wine must be put in new bottles. They became new creation men."[3] Kenneth Copeland echoes this concept of salvation when he says, "We should take the name of Jesus and drive out this sin consciousness. ..A good example [of sin consciousness] is ,'Well, I'm just an old sinner saved by grace.' No, you were an old sinner, you got saved by grace! Now, you are a born-again child of God."[4] This would be confusing to one not versed in the definitions underlying the words "born-again" and "sin consciousness." The latter is any remembrance the believer might have that he sins or has sinned. This is unreality, in Kenyon's system. Believers must only keep in mind their own righteousness, as Copeland says," You need to develop a righteousness consciousness so that you automatically lean on your right-standing with God [not on God]." He continues, "Jesus did this during His earthly ministry. He knew His rights in the kingdom of God and He never hesitated[5]" With this latter quote, his previous meaning becomes clear. Believers must lean on their righteousness, even as Jesus did. Jesus is Perfect Man, the Perfect Adam in human flesh. He is not God Incarnate in human flesh, but a man like every believer, whose Knowledge of His "rights" served Him

76

while on earth. Jesus used this Righteousness, Copeland remarks, because, "Righteousness is an active, powerful force."[6] Believers, along with Jesus and the Apostles, suffer persecution. But, Charles Capps states that, "The Bible says that those who live godly will suffer persecutions. Now, don't go believing for persecution. Actually, they caused most of it because of the foolish things they did!"[7] Capps continues to say that a lack of Knowledge causes failures to prosper and lapses in health. Knowledge is the Gnostic's salvation, that which permits the believer to use forces of faith and righteousness to thwart forces of fear and evil. Copeland adds that it was the "Force of faith controlling [Jesus'] ministry.[8]" Words spoken with Knowledge will release any force, including faith: "The force of Faith is released by words. Faith-filled words put the law of the spirit of life into operation."[9] Do-it-yourself religion has always been attempted by those lacking in the trust to wait for the Lord's timing and perfect Will. His Way is always best, even though the Christian often does not understand all of the reasons behind God's decisions. This is the real virtue of Faith; it trusts when no answer seems to be coming, and in spite of the circumstances. The faithful trust in God, not in their own version of faith to carry them through.

What purpose does Faith, in the Word-Faith doctrine, serve? The main service that "Faith" provides is that of believing in wealth for the believer. The hundredfold return has been preached and taught so often that most Christians have become immune to the basis of Word-Faith claims to that promise. They claim that believers have the authority from Christ to bring all wealth of the world into their possession. As Kenneth Hagin stated in a previous quote, they are demanding of the devil (prince of this world) to release the riches of this world to Word-Faith believers. Using Matthew, chapter 28 (verses 18-20), Gloria Copeland tries to make a case for this position: "Jesus..gave that {His} authority to the believer. 'And Jesus came and spake unto them saying, all power is given unto **Me** in heaven and on earth. Go ye, therefore,... .'"[10] A close search of those verses will not support any giving over of His authority to the believer. Nothing that He said indicates a transfer of authority. Jesus does say that the Christian must go in **His** authority. Any other interpretation is a case of wishful thinking. The same is true of the hundredfold return. The Word-Faith teachings make God into a financial agent, promising an exact hundred times any amount that the believer gives. All that is necessary to bring about this hundredfold is using the force of faith, as Gloria Copeland proclaims, "..The full hundredfold return will come in if we keep our faith active and operating for it."[11] They conclude this because, "God's Word is His Will."[12] Satan's favorite tactic, seen clearly in the Temptations of Christ in the wilderness, is to use God's Word against Him in accusation. Of course, there is always a twist to his interpretations, but Satan knows that the fulfillment of God's Word is in God's Will.

Angelic Forces

Angels are considered to be servants of the
Word-Faith believer. Because of their
status as gods who speak the Word, Angels
are required to obey their commands.
Prosperity is at the heart of these Word-
Faith commands: "If you have 20,000
..[natural men] working to prosper you how
long do you think it would take them to
make you wealthy?"[13] This teacher goes on to
say that angels would prosper the believer
infinitely more than mere natural men. She
continues to use biblical characters to
prove her point: "..The Bible says that
Abraham was extremely rich.."[14] Word-Faith
teachers insist that, "Your words put the
angels to work on your behalf to bring to
pass whatever you say."[15]

His Word is the Sword of His Spirit. The
Holy Spirit guides the Christian in using
God's Word to combat the Enemy and express
the promise of God in faith. With His
guidance, we will never demand that God do
this or that as promised in His Word, apart
from a desire to be utterly yielded to
God's Will and His Way of accomplishing His
Word. In the early church, some were
claiming that the resurrection of the body
had already taken place, or that the anti-
Christ had come. They were severely
reprimanded by Paul, as he encouraged the
church to wait for certain events that were
to signal the real event in time.
Christians of our own day must also
personally live in the presence of the
Father, Son and Spirit daily, so that they
might learn to listen carefully to the
guidance of the Lord in His Word. Going

ahead of God leads to disaster! Going with
Him is the surest way of seeing Him fulfill
His Word in and through us.

The Epistle to the Philippians (3:18-20)
describes the greed of false teachers: "For
many walk, of whom I often told you, and
now tell you even weeping, that they are
enemies of the cross of Christ, whose end
is destruction, whose god is their
appetite, and whose glory is in their
shame, who set their minds ON EARTHLY
THINGS. For our citizenship is in heaven,
from which also we eagerly wait for a
Savior, the Lord Jesus Christ."

Chapter 10

The Unholy Trinity

Heathen concepts of god have at their root the belief in gods who are Good and gods who are evil. Good gods are to be won over with favors and gifts; those who are evil must be placated by blood sacrifices or offerings that subdue their wrath. Gnosticism has heathen concepts which apply to God, Satan and Man. Because of these dualistic viewpoints which reach back into Greek and Persian philosophies and myths, Gnosticism gives to the Christian writings various heathen understandings. Genesis describes the duel of Good and Evil, while a Jealous Creator looks on. Man and Satan are given several different roles, depending on the Gnostic system that is studied. In the new Gnosticism of Kenyon's gospel, Man receives the preeminent status, with the Creator and Satan battling for his attention and favor. These three, the Creator, Man and Satan, form an Unholy Trinity of deities, each with his own realms of power and limitations. Man is perceived as spirit, and as spirit, is equal with God. Copeland explains, "Man was created to function on God's level. Adam walked on that level in the Garden of Eden; but when he disobeyed God, he fell from his position of fellowship and oneness with God. It took Jesus coming to earth as a man to reclaim the authority that Adam

gave over to Satan. ...as a born again
believer, you have the same spiritual
capacity that Jesus has." [1] Because Man is
only spirit, moving about in a physical
body, Man functions like God, they say,
"Your spirit is just as big as God's
because you are born of Him. My son has
the same capacity for strength that I
have." [2]

In Word-Faith teaching, very little is said
about the Holy Trinity, Father, Son and
Holy Spirit. The main focus of their
attention is Man, who he is and how he can
control his world. To replace the Holy
Trinity, a powerful three-some of actors in
the drama of redemption - Man, Creator, and
Satan- dominate the mythology of Word-Faith
teaching. The spiritual realm of control
for each member in the unholy trinity has
strict boundaries that cannot be infringed
upon by the other two. For example,
Copeland mentions limitations of God and
Man in his description of Jesus' born-again
experience in Hell: "Satan ushered
Jesus..into the depths of hell...In Hell,
he suffered death for you and me. The
Bible says Hell was made for Satan and his
angels. ....It was not made for men. Satan
was holding the Son of God there illegally.
God could not [nor could Man] go into hell
as it was not His domain." [3] Notice the
change from calling Jesus "man" to using
the phrase, "Son of God." (The reader
should be warned that Kenyon and his
followers use phrases without real meaning
in striving to use acceptable terminology.
For instance, "Hell was not made for Man,"
becomes the important phrase upon which his
other comments rest.) The Creator is

helpless during the Fall of Man in Word-
Faith mythology. As in so many cases,
everything that happens in scripture
becomes a "law," in this teaching:
"..according to the Law of Genesis, Man
takes on the Nature of His father or lord.
God was Man's spiritual Father; but when
Adam disobeyed God and bowed his knee to
Satan, he changed spiritual fathers...and
at that point, all dominion and authority
[that] God had given him was handed over to
Satan. Suddenly, God was on the outside,
looking in." [4] Creator God was on the
"outside" of this action, having previously
given His authority over the earth to Adam,
or so goes the story. The Creator is a
limited god, looking on at a set of
circumstances out of his control. For this
same reason, Satan is called, by Word-Faith
teachings, the "renegade outlaw" of the
Universe. He, too, is out of Creator-God's
control, beyond his scope of authority.
Man can and will control Satan, however,
according to his Knowledge, as Kenyon
supposes. By speaking scripture and
standing on his godship as a New Creation,
the believer controls both Good and Evil.
The biggest sin in Gnostic thought is
Ignorance: "Ignorance has robbed us of
God's best and kept us below the standard
of life God desires for us to have." [5] And
through speaking words, these teachers
claim to create things out of nothing:
"Your heart is a clearing house. The only
way things can come out of your heart is
through your mouth. First, you speak it
forth, then your words and actions license
a spiritual agency to bring into existence
what you say. There are two spiritual
agencies functioning in the earth: one is

headed by Satan, the other is headed by Jesus."[6]

It is important to comment that every word that comes out of the pen or mouth of a Word-Faith teacher does not carry the same weight. They will often use phrases right out of Christianity, as do other cults, and yet, the phrases are assigned no place in the context, or they are given different meaning. Grace means Ability, for instance. Prayer means Confessing or Affirming the results that the believer desires. It is vital that the Christian be aware that exclamations about the Deity of Christ simply are not borne out by any of the rest of Word-Faith teachings. It is a case of mistaken identity - what seems to be said is not being said at all. As in most philosophies, the reader must look carefully to ascertain what phrases are "building blocks" of the system of thought, and what phrases are simply there to comfort the reader who has traditional viewpoints.

Since Man is equal with God as a spirit in this teaching, he can walk in the "God-kind of Faith," the "love of God," the "life of God," all of which are separated out and available to any God-kind of being like Man. Walking in the love of God, for instance, means walking in another "law:" "Love is the cardinal law of God - and it never fails. Put the love of God into operation and you will succeed."[7] This love becomes a Force which brings favor to the believer apart from God, "By walking in God's love, you release a force to work in your behalf - a force stronger than any force in existence."[8] The New Creation is also equal with God, having been reinstated into God's Class by receiving God's own Nature; he cannot sin. Sin is always qualified with phrases that belie its serious quality: "Now, when you **stumble** and then turn from that sin, He is ready to forgive and cleanse you." Again, since believers cannot really sin, forgiveness is no issue: "'My little children, these things write I unto you, that ye sin not' (1 John 2:1). Notice what John said would keep you free from sin. He said it is the things that he writes or the Word."[9] The writer asserts that the actual words of the verse are to be the cleansing for believers! Another comment from the same source indicates a weak definition of sin for believers: "You are a new creation created in Christ Jesus unto good works. If you **miss the mark** and sin because of the weakness of your flesh, you can receive forgiveness from God. ..When you act on the Word, that is when you are forgiven![10]" Sin is relegated to Evil Flesh, not rooted in a rebellious or disobedient heart. However, Christians know that even after salvation, our hearts need conforming to the Mind of Christ and His Will. The Christian must decide to Sin, although there is a weakness in his members that may draw him into temptation. Ultimately, Sin is an act of the will.

Paul always preached Christ, "and Him Crucified." This might be puzzling for the Twentieth Century Christian, but no one can be drawn to the Gospel of Jesus Christ without coming to Jesus, the One Who physically bore our Sin. He is the only

One Who can forgive us; He paid the price for each and every one who comes to Him for salvation. The Word-Faith gospel has no Cross or Crucified Lord. It only has a dead Christ and a living mortal man who has been called "god." Others have tried to avoid the Cross because they don't want to be identified with a crucified Lord. "The Cross by which I am crucified to the world and the world to me," causes everything but Christ to fall away into insignificance. Material things are no longer important; status in the eyes of friends or enemies fades into a longing to please God, not men. One Word-Faith teacher exclaimed in a seminar, that he couldn't accept the Gospel preached by poor men who had no outward signs of success. But, he continued to say, when Word-Faith teachers came with their teaching of success, he was instantly converted. Now, this same teacher holds "Success Seminars," which are disguised with Christian terminology. He and other Word-Faith proponents flash jewelry and silk shirts in an effort to show that their confession of "Faith" is really working for them! They have missed the Crucified Lord Jesus, and chosen a glittery gospel of the world which says, " you can have it all!" Another example of a desire for the acclaim of men is that of a group of church leaders in a small city in Southern California. They were busily confessing their prosperity, and in order to show their utter confidence, they "acted" like prosperous men and took a limosine to the church banquet. This was supposed to attract wealth, according to Word-Faith claims. Another phrase : "We're King's Kids" has caught the imagination of some

Christians. It has become an excuse to wine and dine in the finest hotels and restaurants available. Christians who act like this would be ashamed to follow a Jesus Who had no place to lay His Head. The Love of Christ takes away the desire for these things. If the desire is still present after the born-again experience, it is a sign that perhaps the flesh is still in control in certain areas. Jesus knew that some disciples were following Him just to have something to eat every day. After feeding five thousand by multiplying food, some continued to seek Him for more: "Jesus answered and said, "Truly truly, I say to you, you seek Me, not because you saw signs, but because you ate of the loaves, and were filled. Do not work for the food which perishes, but for the food which endures to eternal life, which the Son of Man shall give to you.." (John 6:26-27). Signs were given to point the people to Jesus, and still are today. However, seeking Him for material things has no place in the disciple of Jesus Christ.

Chapter 11

The Scriptural View
of Atonement

Christ and Adam

The differences between Adam and Jesus Christ are clearly stated in the scriptures, especially in First Corinthians (Chapter 15:47) " The first man is from the earth, earthy; the second man is from heaven." One, Adam, was from earth and the other, Jesus, came down from Heaven. Kenyon's assertions that both Adam and Christ were equal in that they were Perfect Man are not in any way scriptural. Physical death came through Adam's disobedience, with spiritual estrangement from God and the need to be regenerated through Grace. Physical Resurrection comes through Jesus Christ, Who reconciles Man with God and ends the estrangement with adoption as sons in Him. The contention in Word-Faith teaching that death was not physical is not so because, obviously, Adam died. Bishop Irenaeus wrote in the First-Century that death was a blessing from God because it ended Man's sojourn away from God's presence. Through death, the Christian enters into heavenly fellowship with God. The martyrs faced death joyfully for this reason. They were sure of their hope based on One Who had met death and conquered it in Resurrection. Scripture says that (1 Cor.15: 21-22),"For since by a man came death, by a man also came the resurrection of the dead. For as in Adam

all die, so also in Christ all shall be
made alive."(NASB) Like every sign that
Jesus did, in this case, His Resurrection,
reflects His authority over Sin and Satan.
His Resurrection was also the Seal of the
Father's acceptance of His Pure Offering
for Sin which satisfied God's wrath against
the unholiness of Sin.

The Pure Offering

In the Sacrifices of the Old Testament, the
sins of the repentant were placed
vicariously on the animal to be offered.
The animal, most especially seen in the
unblemished Passover Lamb, had no
imperfections. These were all types of the
purity of the Son of God as a spotless
offering for our Sin on the Cross. To
those who will lay their sins upon Him and
ask forgiveness, He will give forgiveness
and newness of life. Old things will pass
away, and all things will become new! His
own Righteousness covers our sinfulness,
and we are acceptable to the Father. But
the Offering must have the sins placed upon
Him with the consent of the one who has
sinned. Only then, does that Offering
stand in for the sinner. This was true of
the types of the Old Testament, in which
the sinner paid for the animal to be
offered and in some way symbolically laid
the sin upon it. It is certainly true in
the New Covenant of Jesus Christ. Both
Covenants had Sin-Offerings - the former
covenant was the shadow of the Cross and
the New was the fulfillment of the Blood
Sacrifices in the Old. Jesus' Blood was
poured out for our sins. As First Peter
states , (2:22-24) "{He} Who committed no

sin, nor was any deceit found in His mouth; and while being reviled, He did not revile in return; while suffering, He uttered no threats, but kept entrusting Himself to Him who judges righteously; And He Himself bore our sins IN HIS BODY ON THE CROSS, that we might die to sin and live to righteousness; for by His wounds you were healed.(NASB)" And again, in the Book of Hebrews (10:10), we are taught that "..we have been sanctified through the offering of the BODY OF JESUS CHRIST once for all." (NASB) His body and blood were the offerings for our sins, even as He foretold during the Last Supper. Luke's Gospel records the words of Jesus:(22:19)"This is My body which is given for you.." (NASB) The Life is in the Blood, and it is by this Blood that the Life of Jesus Christ cleanses and heals us from Sin and brings us into adopted sonship with the Father. There is no basis for Kenyon's theory that Jesus had to be Born Again spiritually because of the Sin that was laid upon Him. He did NOT become a sinner, nor did He obey Satan. This would have rendered His Offering impure, and denied His Divinity completely. A more devilish concept has not been invented or perpetrated on the public than this concept of Kenyon's! When Jesus said in the Garden, "Not My Will, but Thine be done!" He certainly was not speaking to Satan. Jesus remained obedient to His Father, even though the wrath of God was to be poured out upon Him on behalf of sinful Mankind. Another indication that Jesus held Himself apart from the rest of Mankind was that He said, "You must be born-again," not "We must be born-again!" Christ, therefore, accomplished propitiation for Man's Sin,

redemption   from   that   Sin,   and
reconciliation to God for those who would
come to Him for forgiveness.

The Grace of God

An Eternal God is not easy for humans to
speak about; He enters our time and space
environment,   and   yet,   He   has   seen
everything and knows all things before they
ever occur in time. His Grace goes before
AND   after   those   who believe in His
salvation through Christ. The Covenant to
Abraham is to all who believe the promises
of God. The Law was given to show the
futility of trying to come to the Lord with
works or our own perfection. In Ephesians,
(2:8-9) Paul explains that salvation-faith
is a gift of Grace: "For by grace you have
been saved through faith; and that not of
yourselves, it is the gift of God; not as a
result of works, that no one should boast."
The pharisees tried to use scripture to
prove their own understanding of God and
not to hear from God what He has to say.
Jesus described the situation of their
hearts perfectly in the Gospel of John
(5:39-40),"You   search   the   Scriptures,
because you think that in them you have
eternal life; and it is these that bear
witness of Me; and you are unwilling to
come to Me, that you may have life." (NASB)
Coming to Jesus Christ personally, and
getting   to   know   Him   through   daily
fellowship and prayer is the way to a sure
understanding of what is written in the
Word of God. Without this relationship, it
becomes an end in itself - or worse, a way
to justify non-Christian doctrines   and
disciplines. Scripture becomes a series of

laws in Kenyon's gospel. Law denies Grace;
Man is dependent upon God for Grace, but he
can depend upon himself for the keeping of
the Law. Paul writes (Galatians 2:19)"I do
not nullify the grace of God; for if
righteousness comes through the Law, then
Christ died needlessly."(NASB) Christ kept
the Law perfectly while a Man, in order to
fulfill all its requirements; then, He died
in order that the Grace of salvation could
be made available to each one who comes to
Him for forgiveness. Following the Law -
any Law that claims to lead to holiness and
righteousness - nullifies the Cross of
Christ and the Grace of God.

Chapter 12

Personal Notes

The affluence of the world which surrounds Christians in America, makes the church and ministries susceptible to that same affluence. It can become an acceptable expression of God's blessing. Movie and recording personalities tell their testimonies of conversion to Christ, often without the testimony of a changed life-style and maturity in walking with Christ. Christian ministers fall prey to some, even in their own congregations, who wish to gift them with expensive housing or cars without thought of the scandal it creates for those who are weak in the faith (see I Cor. 9-12, Romans 14:21), and especially for those in the world who know all to well that Christians are supposed to be UNworldly. The pastor would say that these amenities of life are simply gifts from those who want to do something for him. Perhaps those gifts could, instead, be in the form of monetary donations for use by those who are in need of food or housing in his church. Let us do as the early church did, and translate our "things" into money for the needy of the church which can be dispensed by the pastor and the elders. If the Apostle Paul would not even eat meat in front of one who was fearful that the meat had been offered to idols, how much more should those of us in Christian ministries be careful of idols in our testimony of a life crucified to the world? The Word-Faith teaching has promoted these attitudes of worldly wealth for the church. Through it, many pastors have fallen for the message of wealth, and have made a shipwreck of their faith.

Talk-Show Testimonies

It is hard to forget the Larry Flynt "testimony of conversion" not many years ago. Some Christian talk-show hosts rushed to his side, without discernment from the Holy Spirit or waiting for the fruits of his conversion to show in a change of pornographic life-style. The change never did take place. Religious "experiences" without mention of Jesus Christ, some based on visions, can be diabolical delusions or, at the very least, products of active minds. James' Epistle urges the church not to show partiality toward the wealthy or famous: (2:1-6) "My brethren, do not hold your faith in our glorious Lord Jesus Christ with an attitude of personal favoritism. For if a man comes into your assembly with a gold ring and dressed in fine clothes, and there also comes in a poor man in dirty clothes, and you pay special attention to the one who is wearing the fine clothes, and say, 'You sit here in a good place,' and you say to the poor man, 'You stand over there, or sit down by my footstool,' have you not made distinctions among yourselves, and become judges with EVIL MOTIVES? Listen, my beloved brethren: did not God choose the poor of this world to be rich in faith and heirs of the kingdom which He promised to those who love

Him? But you have dishonored the poor man. Is it not the rich who oppress you and personally drag you into court?"(NASB) It is tempting to translate two of the above verses into thoroughly modern English, with the phrases, "Sit here in a good place in front of the television camara," and "Stand over there in the viewing audience." In any case, the meaning is clear from the scriptures.

These attitudes are the same as those belonging to the children of this world. In First John (4:3-5), the Holy Spirit indicates that the spirit of antichrist is in the false prophets who have gone out from the church into the world. Therefore, the world listens to them and understands their teaching. However, the world will never comprehend the Gospel of the Crucified Lord Jesus. Christians should perhaps wonder when the world flocks to "giant" cathedrals and churches, televised throughout the nation, which major in personalities and not the Gospel. Jesus is out of place - the Crucified Lord has been traded in for the glittering gospel of "What looks good must BE good." The Cross is a stumbling block to unbelievers. The Way through Christ to God is narrow; Christians cannot be fooled into believing that everyone can easily accept the Gospel of One Who had no place to lay His Head. The words that Jesus directed to those desiring to follow Him are harsh by our standards, but He was speaking the Truth! He said "Sell all and follow Me." Possessions replace God in most of our lives before commitment to Christ, and these must be replaced by the Lord. He does not stand for idolatry of any kind. Those in ministry, in servanthood to the Body of Christ, are especially visible to the scrutiny of their flock and to that of the world.

Media Massage

A local Christian televison station has christened Kenneth Hagin, "Dad Hagin," in recent months. The last three or four years have brought an increasing acceptance by this station and its affiliates of Word-Faith doctrines of prosperity. One pastor from the Midwest was recently a guest on their evening program. After his interview, this writer spoke with him about his experience. He had given solid, scriptural bases in rebuttal of Word-Faith teachings and used his extensive, pastoral experience as a format for his firm rejection of its assumptions. He pointed out during his interview that night, that Word-Faith teachings had seriously hampered many of his church members by placing on them a heavy burden of condemnation and confusion regarding healing and the place of Christ in their lives. His comments were met with scepticism and obvious disbelief on the part of the host. At the end of the interview, the host said, with an air of finality, that no matter what anyone said, he would continue to "claim things for God's Kingdom," or words to that effect. He indicated, by saying this, that the Word-Faith teachings would continue to be a part of their television programming and their belief-system. After this comment by the host, wild applause came loudly over the airwaves, implying complete acceptance of his statement by those in the studio audience. However, according to this pastor, the television audience heard nothing from a studio audience. The loud applause was "canned;" the engineer had played a tape of applause. This is a sad commentary on the methods which are used to provide a forum of unconditional acceptance for the Word-Faith teachings. It's clearly time to open our windows, and let the winds of the Holy Spirit winnow the chaff from among the teachings presented in our Christian churches and media.

Apostasy and Antichrist

The great falling away from Christ and His Body, the church, is one sign of the nearness of the person of Antichrist. Antichrist is a topic of discussion, but very little mention is made of references to the great apostasy. Perhaps the parable of the wheat and tares (Matt. 13:24-30) would fit the description of this apostasy, as the Lord purifies His Bride before His coming for the church in the Rapture. The parable points to false believers who must be taken out of the fellowship of believers. At the time of the harvest, the tares will be gathered up first, indicating that the falling away will happen just before the harvesting of the "wheat" - true believers - at the time of the catching away of the Christians. The church will be purged of false apostles and false prophets. As Paul writes to the Thessalonians (II Thes. 2:3), "Let no one in any way deceive you, for it [the Day of the Lord] will not come unless the apostasy

comes first, and the man of lawlessness is
revealed, the son of destruction,.." (NASB)
Evidently, some were saying that the Day of
the Lord had already occurred. There are
various interpretations of these words, but
most would agree that it refers to a
falling away from the church - not of
believers, but of those who seemed to be
believers in Jesus Christ. And so, every
true believer says with his whole heart,
"Come, Lord Jesus!"

End Notes

CHAPTER ONE

References here are from "Against Heresy," by Irenaeus,(Oxford: James Parker & Co., 1872).

CHAPTER TWO

CHAPTER THREE

1. E. W. Kenyon,"Jesus the Healer," (Lynwood, Washington: Kenyon Gospel Publishing Society, 19th ed., 1968), p. 6.
2. Ibid., p. 5.

CHAPTER FOUR

1. Kenyon, "The Wonderful Name of Jesus," (Lynnwood, Wash.: Kenyon's Gospel Publishing, 20th ed.,1964), p. 201.
2. Kenyon, "What Happened From the Cross to the Throne," (Lynnwood, Wash.: Kenyon's Gospel Publishing, n.d.) pp. 44-45.
3. Ibid., p.43.
4. Kenneth Copeland, "What Happened from the Cross to the Throne," (Fort Worth: The Believer's Bible Course Tape Series, #00-0303).
5. Gloria Copeland, "God's Will for You," (Fort Worth: Kenneth Copeland Publications,1972) p.5.
6. K. Copeland, op. cit.
7. Ibid.

CHAPTER FIVE

1. Kenyon, "Two Kinds of Life," (Lynnwood, Wash.:Kenyon's Gospel Publishing, 6th ed., 1971), p.39.
2. Jerry Savelle, "The Established Heart," (Tulsa: Harrison House, 1977), p.15.
3. Kenneth Hagin, "Faith Food," (Tulsa: Kenneth Hagin Ministries, 4th ed.,1979), p. 23.
4. Kenyon, "What Happened from the Cross to the Throne," p.23.
5. Ibid., p. 82.
6. Savelle, op. cit., p. 15.
7. Kenyon, "Two Kinds of Life," p. 45.
8. Kenyon, "The Blood Covenant," p. 53.
9. Kenyon, "What Happened from the Cross to the Throne," p. 84.
10. Ibid., p. 76.
11. Kenyon, "New Creation Realities, " (Lynnwood, Wash.: Kenyon's Gospel Publishing Society, 7th ed., 1964) p. 35.
12. Kenyon, "The Hidden Man," (Lynnwood, Wash.: Kenyon's Gospel Publishing Society, 8th ed., 1970), p.197.

CHAPTER SIX

1. Charles Capps, "The Tongue, A Creative Force," (Tulsa: Harrison House, 1976) pp. 32-33.
2. Kenyon, "Jesus the Healer," p. 23.
3. Kenyon, "Two Kinds of Life," p. 18.
4. Kenyon, "Blood Covenant," p. 30.
5. Ibid., p. 54.

6. Kenneth Copeland, "A Ceremony of Marriage," Communion Service.(Fort Worth: Kenneth Copeland Ministries, Inc., 1979).
7. Kenyon, "Jesus the Healer," p. 26.
8. Kenneth Hagin, "Training the Human Spirit," (Tape)
9. Kenneth Copeland, "The Laws of Prosperity," (Fort Worth: Copeland Publications, 1974), pp. 64-65.

CHAPTER SEVEN

1. Kenyon, "The Wonderful Name of Jesus," p. 16.
2. Ibid., p. 11.
3. Kenyon, "The Hidden Man," p. 206.
4. Ibid., p. 212.
5. Kenyon, "The Wonderful Name..," p. 22.
6. Kenyon, "The Hidden Man," p. 214.
7. Kenyon, "New Creation Realities," p. 92.
8. Ibid., p. 12.
9. Charles Capps, "Can Your Faith Fail?" (Tulsa: Harrison House, 1976), pp. 27-28.
10. Kenyon, "New Creation Realities," p. 28.
11. Kenyon, "What Happened from the Cross to the Throne," p. 104.
12. Gloria Copeland, "Believer's Voice of Victory Broadcast," (Trinity Broadcasting Network, Tustin, CA,) April 2, 1981.
13. Charles Capps, "The Tongue..," p. 132.
14. Kenyon, "What Happened..," p. 99.
15. Ibid., p. 102.
16. Capps, "The Tongue..," p. 34.

17. Savelle, op. cit., p. 9.
18. Kenyon, "New Creation Realities," p. 15.
19. Kenyon, "The Hidden Man," p. 36.

CHAPTER EIGHT

1. Gloria Copeland, "And Jesus Healed Them All," (Fort Worth: Kenneth Copeland Ministries, 1981), p. 18.
2. Kenneth Hagin, "Training the Human Spirit," (Tape)
3. Kenyon, "The Blood Covenant," p. 53.
4. Kenyon, "New Creation..," p. 72.
5. Kenyon, "Two Kinds of Life," p. 15.
6. G. Copeland, op. cit., p. 15.
7. Ibid.
8. Ibid., p. 17.
9. Kenneth Hagin, "Faith Food," (Winter), p. 58.
10. G. Copeland, op. cit., p. 13.
11. Ibid.

CHAPTER NINE

1. G. Copeland, "God's Will Is Prosperity," (Tulsa: Harrison House, 1978), p. 8.
2. Capps, "The Tongue..," p. 132.
3. Ibid., p. 126.
4. K. Copeland, "The Force of Righteousness," (Fort Worth: Copeland Publications, n.d.), pp. 9-11.
5. Ibid., pp. 10-11.
6. Ibid., p. 11.
7. Capps, "Can Your Faith Fail?" p. 14.
8. K. Copeland, "The Force of Faith,"

(Fort Worth: Copeland Publications,   n.d.)
p. 12.
    9. Ibid., p. 18.
    10. G. Copeland, op. cit., p. 48.
    11. Ibid., p. 59.
    12. Ibid., p. 69, 97.
    13. G. Copeland, op. cit., p.92.
    14. Ibid., p.93.
    15. Ibid., p.94.

CHAPTER TEN

    1. K. Copeland, "Walking in the Realm
of the Miraculous," (Fort Worth: Kenneth
Copeland Ministries, n.d.), p. 15.
    2. Ibid., p. 16.
    3. Ibid., p. 77.
    4. K. Copeland, "Our Covenant With
God," (Fort Worth: Kenneth Copeland
Ministries, 1976), p. 8.
    5. K. Copeland, "Walking in the
Realm..," p. 16.
    6. Ibid., p. 36.
    7. Ibid., p. 15.
    8. Ibid., p. 32.
    9. Believer's Voice of Victory
Magazine, Vol. 12, No. 1, p.3.
    10. Ibid., p. 10.

CHAPTER ELEVEN

CHAPTER TWELVE

Recommended Reading

Irenaeus. "Against Heresy." Oxford: James Parker & Co., 1872.

Jonas, Hans. "The Gnostic Religion; message of the alien god and the beginning of Christianity;" Boston: Beacon Press, 1958.

Pagels, Elaine. "The Gnostic Gospels." New York: Random House, 1979.

Smithalls, Walter. "Gnosticism in Corinth." Abingdon Press, 1971.

Van Groningen, G. "First Century Gnosticism; Its Origins and Motifs." Leiden, E. J. Brill, 1967.

Mansel, Henry. "The Gnostic Heresies of the First and Second Centuries." London: John Murig Publishers, 1875.

Wilson, Robert McL. "The Gnostic Problem; A Study of the Relationship between Hellenistic Judaism and the Gnostic Heresy." London: A.K. Mowbray, 1958.